Daas Torah Series

Child & Domestic Abuse

Compact Practical Guide

Daas Torah Series

Child & Domestic Abuse

Compact Practical Guide

Volume III

Daniel Eidensohn

Emunah Press
Jerusalem – New York
2011

Child & Domestic Abuse III
Compact Practical Guide

© 2011 by Daniel Eidensohn
All rights reserved

This book may not be reproduced in whole or part in any form (beyond that which is permitted by the Copyright Law and except by reviews for the public press) without written permission from the copyright holder. Violation of this prohibition constitutes stealing - both in Torah and secular sources.

Much time and effort went into producing this book.

yadmoshe@gmail.com

http://daattorah.blogspot.com
Phone: 347 560 4083

My previous works are **Yad Moshe** (Index to Igros Moshe of Rav Moshe Feinstein), **Yad Yisroel** (Index to Mishna Berura) and **Daas Torah** (A sourcebook of Jewish thought). **Child & Domestic Abuse Volumes I & II**

DEDICATION - Mrs. Judy Young A"H

This sefer is about the realization - that for a person to deal with the serious issues in life - it is not enough to have faith in G-d and Torah. Even when this faith is combined with a comprehensive system of Halachic or community leaders and rabbis - it is not enough to be able to produce a viable society. Making a meaningful contribution to helping others and improving the world doesn't follow automatically from growing up, being smart and talented, becoming educated or even developing a sophisticated knowledge of the rules of society. Society doesn't automatically protect its own – even those who are insiders or the leaders of the system.

The missing ingredients that a person needs to bring about an improvement of the world (tikun olam) and serve G-d's purpose in this world (Avodas Hashem) are: 1) a tremendous love of one's fellow man, 2) commonsense (yashrus), 3) an overwhelming sense of responsibility to do whatever is needed to help others in distress – without regard to personal cost and 4) faith in G-d and prayer.

My late sister-in-law – Mrs. Judy Young – was such a person.

Judy was the daughter of the distinguished Rabbi and Mrs. Maurice Lamm, who were her role models in Torah, Chesed and Jewish leadership. She was a rare individual: she was a born leader, intelligent, energetic, charismatic, and had a warm, caring personality. She would teach not only by words but also by example of love, of chesed, and ma'asim tovim, guiding her students in all facets of their lives. This made her an inspiring teacher and innovative educator, who influenced the lives of thousands and brought them closer to Torah.

She worked tirelessly in outreach and education. She was the Torah Studies principal at Machon Academy, a kiruv high school for Bukharian girls in Queens, New York. She was one of the founders, and the guiding light, of the Amein Group, in Lawrence, New York, that has inspired hundreds of women. Judy was a much sought after inspirational speaker, lecturing for prominent kiruv institutions including Neve Yerushalayim, Aish HaTorah, Ohr Somayach and Gateways. Judy gave life-altering small classes to women on being a Jewish wife and mother. She established women's education programs in Los Angeles, and then in Atlanta, and then in New York, that affected hundreds of women and their families.

And, most important of all, she was a devoted wife to her husband Rabbi Yitzchok Young, a superlative mother to her seven children, and a devoted, loving grandmother.

This is just a short synopsis of her accomplishments in her full life of fifty years. All of this, despite the fact that she battled and conquered cancer three times and was told by her doctors that she would never have children.

May her memory be a blessing.

PREFACE

CAUTION – CONSULT YOUR RABBI & THERAPIST

It is important to be fully aware that I am just presenting the halachos in translation and have arranged them in a framework that I think is optimal for dealing with the topic of this sefer - abuse. I am not a posek but simply a researcher and organizer of halachos. However as Rav Sternbuch has told me, "The classic sources do not need a haskoma!"

I think that you will agree that the halachos presented in this sefer are clear and readily understood. They are not arcane and esoteric doctrines which can only be understood by a genius who has immersed himself exclusively in the study of halacha for many years. Furthermore I am following the guidelines that Rav Eliashiv gave me for my previous sefer, "What you are presenting are not minority opinions or views taken from obscure or questionable sources." The halachic views presented here are mainstream views of the major poskim from the Talmudic period to modern times.

On the other hand, I think this is the first time that many of these halachic views have been collected and applied in an organized fashion to the issue of child abuse. It is also clear that this compendium of halacha shows that there is no inherent conflict between halacha and commonsense. There is no inherent conflict between halacha and the recommendations of mental health professionals and secular law as to what needs to be done to protect against abuse. The reason for this compatibility is that I utilized the view expressed by Rav Moshe Sternbuch, Rav Yehuda Silman and others that abuse issues are simply issues of defending oneself and others from harm. Therefore a full judicial investigation is not needed to determine whether he is guilty of transgressing arcane halachos which are only understood by major poskim and which the rabbis today have no power to enforce. According to the perspective of defense - it is simply necessary to ask," What needs to be done to protect against abuse and abusers?"

However, it is important that each individual, well in advance of needing them, discuss these issues with his rabbi or posek to make sure that they are properly understood. That is because these issues are matters of life and death – figuratively and literally. Similarly, an expert in abuse needs to be consulted.

Besides the halachos, I have also provided the latest facts and views of the mental health workers and legal experts who deal with this problem. The real concern in this area is not misunderstanding the halacha - but rather misunderstanding fully the reality of abuse. As Rav Sternbuch told me, "A posek first asks what are the facts before he asks what is the halacha." Applying a correct understanding of halacha to an incorrect understanding of the facts – is a recipe for disaster! Therefore even a rabbi who is totally familiar with the halachic material I have presented – might lack a full understanding of the nature of an abuser and the horrific consequences of his actions.

Abuse is a very complex issue

This book is not a catalogue of the manifestations of the crime of abuse and a listing of solutions. The problem of abuse requires a greater sensitivity and knowledge regarding the dignity of an individual within the context of society. It ultimately requires understanding psychology and sociology and law. But that is still not sufficient. Each individual needs to develop an understanding of what the Will of G-d is as manifested through the Torah as interpreted by Torah scholars over a period of thousands of years. The knowledge of each part informs and prepares for an understanding of the others. The book requires not just a reader but rather a fully engaged participant who consults a variety of experts in his community.

Purpose of Volume III Compact Practical Guide

This volume provides the basic information necessary to understand the Jewish prohibition of abuse and the obligations required to prevent it and to help the victim. It consists of a sampling of the material contained in volume I and II of Child and Domestic Abuse. It contains the most important concepts and sources but it does not have the essays written by experts describing the nature of abuse and it lacks the depth of primary sources. It contains only 150 pages instead of 900.

Content of Volumes I and II

Volume I and II each constitute a complete work and yet they clearly supplement each other.

Volume I

1. Overview & summary survey the major issues of abuse as well providing a concise summary of practical concerns. It includes an **Introduction**, **Practical Guide**, **Protocols of Orthodox Organizations** for dealing with abuse and a **Synopsis** of the halachic and psychological issues that was reviewed and annotated by Rav Sternbuch. It also has chapters describing a number of actual abuse cases - including those written by survivors of abuse.

2. The Essays provide in depth analysis of a variety topics by experts (rabbis, psychotherapists and lawyers) who share their knowledge and experience on critical issues.

Volume II

3. Translated Sources arranged by Topic is a comprehensive collection of Jewish legal sources that are organized according to topic for quick access on the major issues. These texts concern the need to protect the individual as well as his right to protect himself. It contains many texts related to child and domestic abuse, rabbinic authority, the relationship between Jewish and secular law and authority, and the Jewish view of sexuality and deviance. It is indispensable for those who wish to learn and understand the original legal sources. It also serves as a convenient and accessible reference for rabbis who wish to review and refresh their understanding. Lawyers, community leaders and psychologists will also find it useful to understand the parameters of legitimate response when developing strategies to deal with the problem. The third section presents the accepted mainstream views on the topic – including the authoritative writings of the major contemporary authorities.

4. Rabbinic Sources section is comprised of more complete citations of the material cited in the book. They are arranged by name rather than by topic. They are presented here for convenience of those who remember the author of the citation but not the section where the citation is quoted. It is also valuable because often only a part of the material was mentioned in the book.

5. Original Hebrew texts are provided in endnotes to the translation.

TABLE OF CONTENTS

DEDICATION - Mrs. Judy Young a"h i

PREFACE ii

    CAUTION – CONSULT YOUR RABBI & THERAPIST ii

    Abuse is a very complex issue iii

    Purpose of Volume III Compact Practical Guide iii

    Content of Volumes I and II iv

TABLE OF CONTENTS v

INTRODUCTION 9

    Contribution of HaRav Moshe Sternbuch, shlita 9

    Halachic first priority is to help victim 9

    Victim is not sacrificed to protect others 10

    Spousal abuse - defined 10

    Child sexual abuse – defined 11

    Dealing with abuse is complex & requires experts 11

    Blind outrage can be as destructive as silence 12

    Yaakov & Dinah - outrage vs. restrained silence 12

    Lack of evidence is not proof of innocence 13

    Not every sin is explicitly stated in Shulchan Aruch 13

    All abuse is harmful – even if it is not a capital offense 14

    Commonsense is a Torah obligation 14

    Awareness of consequences of abuse is recent 15

Earliest responsa of child abuse are from 1850's *19*
Change results from knowledge of the harm of abuse *20*
Betrayal by family & authorities is also abuse *20*
Major paradigm shift in Orthodox community *21*
Shameful to talk about abuse - but so is denying it *22*

Mayo Clinic Report on Pedophilia (2007) **24**
Effects of abuse on children *24*
Number of victims per molester & amount of abuse *24*
Treatment *24*
Recidivism Rate *25*

*Two halachic frameworks – defensive vs. judicial **27**
By Rav Yehuda Silman *27*

Guidelines of Orthodox Organizations **29**
Association of Jewish Camp Operators - 2006 .... *29*
Suggested cover letter to parents *31*
Things to Tell Your Child Before the Camp Season *32*
Behavioral Standards of Camp Aguda *33*
Vaad harabbonim of Baltimore 2007 .... *35*
Rabbinical Council of America - 2010 .... *39*
Agudath Israel & Torah U'Mesorah *41*
Ohel & Mandated Reporting *45*
Flatbush Shomrim - 2010 .... *46*
Torah u'Mesora: Behavioral standards for educators *48*
Torah u'Mesora: Declaration of Rabbinical Board *49*

*Practical guide of what to do	51
*Synopsis of HaRav Moshe Sternbuch's views	61
Need to investigate all rumors and charges of abuse	*63*
The first thing a real posek asks is, "What are the facts."	*64*
Protection of society sometimes requires emergency laws	*64*
Circumstantial evidence & testimony of women & children	*65*
Mesira (informing) the secular authorities	*65*
Mandatory governmental reporting	*65*
Aiva - causing hatred to Jews - is reason to report abuse	*66*
Consulting rabbi before calling social services or police	*66*
Rejecting a rabbi's psak when he says not to go to the police	*67*
Chemical castration - treatment not punishment	*68*
Social sanctions - burial, aliya or minyan	*68*
Teshuva (repentance) - encourage by not reporting molesting?	*68*
Abortion in the case of rape and incest	*69*
Background checking - Database and fingerprinting	*69*
Jewish calculus – to stop sin or suffering?	71
Excessive fear of sinning prevents helping	73
G-d's reasons for rape and abuse	78
Kiruv can be dangerous to marriage	81
Abused wife's salvation: Waiting for a traffic light	83
Retelling a story of Dr. Naomi Remen	*83*
Lashon harah is sometimes a mitzva	85
*Wife beating is always prohibited	87

Prison is a legitimate punishment 89
Appropriate punishment 89
Free harmful person from jail – redeem captive? 93
Today's prison are not considered life threatening 94

Self-defense against uncertain danger (rodef) 96

Responsa & comments of Gedolim 97
Chasam Sofer (Gittin 7a) – Harassment 97
Pischei Teshuva – lashon harah 98
Rambam – Damage to a community 99
Rav Moshe Sternbuch – dangerous driver 99
Rav Shlomo Zalman Auerbach – child abuse 102
Rav Shmuel Wosner – dangerous driver 102
Rav Yehuda Silman – child abuse 103
Rav Yitzchok Weiss –child abuse 108
Rav Yosef Shalom Eliashiv – child abuse 110
Shulchan Aruch – self defense 115
Tzitz Eliezar – child abuse 118

INTRODUCTION

Contribution of HaRav Moshe Sternbuch, shlita

The idea to write a book about the topic of abuse developed as the result of discussions I have had in the last 3 years with many people – in particular with HaRav Moshe Sternbuch, shlita. He not only has encouraged me to write about and publicize these issues but also nudged me to complete a book on the topic. He is pained by the suffering of abuse victims and is concerned with the widespread ignorance of these matters and the resulting ineffective and harmful responses from well-meaning individuals and communities. While he is fully aware of the shortcomings of the secular institutions in dealing with these matters, he is also concerned by the widespread misunderstandings of Jewish law and ignorance of the actual damage caused by abuse. He recently published a teshuva in which he criticized a principal's claim that he couldn't listen to assertions of abuse because they were only rumors and thus violated the prohibition of lashon harah (tale bearing). The **Synopsis Section** in this book is the result of his suggestion that I write a summary of the issues that we had discussed. He carefully reviewed the resulting summary and wrote comments and corrections – which I have included.

It is important to note that HaRav Moshe Sternbuch, shlita has only reviewed the material of the Synopsis Section but not the rest of the book. Thus the views expressed in the rest of the book are not necessarily his views – except where explicitly stated.

Halachic first priority is to help victim

This book is an attempt to provide a greater awareness of the Torah's view of abuse. It also presents the views of psychology and law. It is not meant as a simplistic cookbook with black and white answers. It is a supplement – not a replacement for consultation with experts in Torah, psychology and law. It attempts to raise awareness of the complexity of this issue. While some of this information is just good commonsense – much of it is not intuitively obvious. It is a book meant not only for rabbis and community leaders – but also parents and victims – as well as mental health professionals and the legal profession. This book was written to be accessible

Child & Domestic Abuse

to people from diverse backgrounds. While a good background in halacha (Jewish law) is desirable to understand this material properly, it is not indispensable.

Victim is not sacrificed to protect others

The primary obligation according to Jewish law is to protect people from harm. That also means helping those who have been harmed and guarding them against future damage. This book cites many sources for this important principle. Rav Sternbuch told me that Jewish law is only secondarily concerned with the collateral damage to individuals, family, schools and community by the reporting of abuse. Innocent victims are not to be left to be abused in order to preserve the reputation and well being of others.

Spousal abuse - defined

(Sources: National Domestic Violence Hotline, National Center for Victims of Crime, and WomensLaw.org)

Domestic violence can be defined as a pattern of abusive behavior in any relationship that is used by one partner to gain or maintain power and control over another intimate partner.

Domestic violence can be physical, sexual, emotional, economic, or psychological actions or threats of actions that influence another person. This includes any behaviors that intimidate, manipulate, humiliate, isolate, frighten, terrorize, coerce, threaten, blame, hurt, injure, or wound someone.

Physical Abuse: Hitting, slapping, shoving, grabbing, pinching, biting, hair-pulling, biting, etc. Physical abuse also includes denying a partner medical care or forcing alcohol and/or drug use.

Sexual Abuse: Coercing or attempting to coerce any sexual contact or behavior without consent. Sexual abuse includes, but is certainly not limited to marital rape, attacks on sexual parts of the body, forcing sex after physical violence has occurred, or treating one in a sexually demeaning manner.

Emotional Abuse: Undermining an individual's sense of self-worth and/or self-esteem. This may include, but is not limited to constant criticism, diminishing one's abilities, name-calling, or damaging one's relationship with his or her children.

Introduction

Economic Abuse: Making or attempting to make an individual financially dependent by maintaining total control over financial resources, withholding one's access to money, or forbidding one's attendance at school or employment.

Psychological Abuse: Causing fear by intimidation; threatening physical harm to self, partner, children, or partner's family or friends; destruction of pets and property; and forcing isolation from family, friends, or school and/or work…

Child sexual abuse – defined

Sexual abuse means to use a child in any way that provides sexual gratification of the adult. This means not only sexual intercourse but also holding or fondling in a way that causes sexual arousal in the adult. It also includes showing pornography to the child as well as discussion of a sexual nature for the purpose of getting the adult sexually aroused. Sexual abuse also means exposing genitals or taking pornographic pictures. It is prohibited whether the child gives his consent, is forced or even if he is unaware of the significance of what he is doing

Dealing with abuse is complex & requires experts

Rabbinical training isn't sufficient

Formal rabbinical training, which primarily studies the laws of kashrus, serves to teach whether a pot is kosher but doesn't prepare a rabbi to deal with a student who claims he/she was molested. Finely-tuned empathy and sensitivity to the plight of those in pain is often useless without expert guidance in the nature of this complex issue. An ability to master the profound insights in the Torah does not necessary provide one with the knowledge of how to handle a colleague who is alleged to be having an affair with a 15 year old student – or a student whose father is having an incestual relationship with her.

Therapist without special training can be harmful

On the other hand, there are therapists who confidently provide therapy or give advice – which is sometimes useless or even harmful. Social workers and police can sometimes be insensitive and cause great damage by their investigations or charges. I still remember the day that a social worker came to my home to investigate a complaint that I was letting my child wildly run around the supermarket without supervision. It took a while to explain that this was impossible as my only child was then 3 months old. People have lost custody of their children and have gone to jail –

Child & Domestic Abuse

because of a misunderstanding of innocent events by neighbors or malicious slander by their enemies. Having a Ph.D. in psychology or having served 15 years on the police force does not automatically qualify a person to deal with these issues.

Blind outrage can be as destructive as silence

While ignoring abuse is obviously harmful, responding with blind outrage and condemnation can also cause damage. Actions - untempered with knowledge and experience - can be just as harmful as silence. A teacher, who innocently pats a student on the back, can find that he and his family are destroyed by unfounded rumors that he is a pedophile. Claims of abuse against a spouse are not uncommonly made by couples engaged in bitter divorce procedures. These claims are used as a vicious tactic to gain more leverage in the legal dispute with their estranged spouse. Even the "objective" questioning of children by social workers or police investigators is fraught with danger because children often have trouble distinguishing between fact and fantasy. There is also the well-known problem of false memories being planted by well meaning questioning. Those who act entirely from outrage often ignore information that questions the truth of the accusations. The uncomfortable reality is that often it is impossible to know exactly what has happened. Furthermore as Rav Moshe Halberstam (Yeshurun 15 page 651) points out, even if a person is in fact guilty of abuse – utmost care need to be taken to minimize harming and degrading his family.

Yaakov & Dinah - outrage vs. restrained silence

When Yaakov's daughter Dinah was raped and abused by their neighbor Shechem – there were two reactions. Yaakov reacted with silence, "And Jacob heard that he had defiled Dinah his daughter; and his sons were with his cattle in the field; and Jacob held his peace until they came." (Bereishis 34:5). Her brothers, however, reacted with outrage, "And the sons of Yaakov came from the field when they heard it; and the men were grieved, and they were very angry, because Shechem had done an outrageous deed in Israel by raping Jacob's daughter; something which should not to be done." (Bereishis 34:7).

Furthermore we see that Yaakov's sons not only expressed anger but they acted on their outrage and killed Shechem and his clan. Yaakov protested against this revenge by saying, "And Yaakov said to [his sons] Shimon and Levi, You have brought trouble on me to make me odious among the inhabitants of the land, among

Introduction

the Canaanites and the Perizzites; and I being few in number, they shall gather together against me, and slay me; and I shall be destroyed, I and my house" (Bereishis 34:30). His sons responded to their father's protest by simply saying, " And they said, Should he deal with our sister as with a harlot?" (Bereishis 34:31).

This illustrates the complexity and conflicts inherent in dealing with sexual abuse. Yaakov wanted to do something but did not because he was very concerned about the danger of retaliation from their neighbors. However, his sons insisted that the possible consequences of retaliation were irrelevant. They insisted that the main concern was that they had to react and punish the perpetrator of this outrage. Rashi (Bereishis 34:25) says that Yaakov's sons did not discuss this matter with their father before they took action. The same issues exist today.

Lack of evidence is not proof of innocence

If insufficient evidence has been found regarding the accusation that someone is a molester – that doesn't mean that the suspect is innocent. So what should be done with the suspect?

According to the "judicial model" (both Jewish and secular) - since there is no case it is equivalent to saying he is innocent. In fact according to Jewish law if there aren't two kosher witnesses - the charges are not allowed to be made public. However according to the "defense against harm" model - the suspected abuser can not be trusted and restrictions or supervisions are necessary.

If he is a teacher or someone who deals with children - he can not be allowed unrestricted access to the children and there are solid grounds for dismissal simply because of the charges. If he is a parent then there needs to be careful monitoring of his children. These are difficult cases to deal with - especially since both sides usually have proponents who feel very strongly that they have the truth.

Not every sin is explicitly stated in Shulchan Aruch

One of the most egregious errors made in dealing with abuse - is to focus entirely on the question of whether the Torah explicitly considers the action a punishable crime. Thus an abuser or his defender might say, "There is no Torah prohibition against molesting a child." Or alternatively, "It is not abuse but rather a consensual relationship if the girl is older than 12 and the boy is older than 13 years old." or "Intercourse with a baby girl below the age of three or a male below the age of nine is not considered a sexual relationship according to the Torah." or "If there is no penetration but just fondling, it is not prohibited." Thus they claim that anything that is not explicitly prohibited by Torah or Rabbinic law is permitted or at least is not a serious sin.

However this is a seriously mistaken understanding of the nature of Torah and mitzvos. The absence of an explicit prohibition does not mean that something is permitted. This mistake is the subject of a major discussion by the Ramban (Vayikra 19:2 /Devarim 6:18). He states that someone can be a menuval (disgusting abomination) even while apparently observing the Torah. That is because the Torah does not explicitly mention every instance of prohibited behavior. He identified meta obligations - such as being holy or being just that are Torah obligations. These govern many behaviors that are not explicit in the Torah. These general principles require commonsense in applying them.

All abuse is harmful – even if it is not a capital offense

Furthermore, an act of abuse doesn't need to be deserving of death or kares in order for it to have serious consequences on the victim. An action needs to be prevented or stopped just because it is harming someone or is disrupting society – not just because it has a severe punishment.

Commonsense is a Torah obligation

R' Yehuda HaChasid (Sefer Chasidim #153): If something is self evident that it should be done - even though it is not specifically commanded - there is a punishment for not doing it…. He should have thought that perhaps something that is obvious might be against the will of G-d.

Rambam (Moreh Nevuchim 3:17): A person is rewarded for any good deed and punished for sin - even though these activities were not commanded by a prophet. This is because a person is held accountable for those things that are dictated by commonsense.

Rabbeinu Nissim Gaon (Introduction to Talmud): The reason that there is punishment for activities not specifically commanded is because all those Mitzvos that are derived from commonsense are obligated on everyone from the day that G-d first created Adam. This obligation is not only for him but also all his descendants afterwards for all generations.

Introduction

Sanhedrin (74a): How did we know that someone is not allowed to kill another to save his own life? It is a sevara (commonsense).

Awareness of consequences of abuse is recent

Severity of abuse consequences was not widely known

Rabbi David Zweibel executive vice president of Agudath Israel of America **The Jewish Daily**, October 10, 2008

"Until not terribly long ago, the issue was very much in the shadows," said David Zwiebel, director of government affairs and general counsel of Agudath Israel of America. "The fact that there were isolated reports here and there of cases arising in yeshiva settings, it was known, but they were very isolated."

"Sometimes they were dealt with correctly and sometimes incorrectly," Zwiebel added, "but the severity of the problem and the possible magnitude were really things that most people, including myself, just didn't understand."

General awareness about abuse began only from 1970's

Encyclopedia Britannica (Child Abuse 2008): Opinions about the scale and nature of child abuse have changed dramatically since the 1960s, and the notion that children are widely subject to abuse and exploitation has become firmly fixed in the public consciousness. Child abuse also has become a major topic of study in academia; themes of incest and abuse are now common in the social and behavioral sciences, as well as in such diverse subjects as literature, social theory, and cultural and women's studies. The surging interest in child abuse, child protection, and children's rights was one of the most significant social developments of the late 20th century.

Encyclopedia Britannica (Child Abuse 2008): Child-protection legislation proliferated during the 1960s. First developed in the United States, these laws soon became models for criminal statutes in many other countries. In 1962, American medical authorities discovered the phenomenon of "baby battering"—the infliction of physical violence on small children—and both the federal government and states adopted laws to investigate and report such acts; eventually, these laws were applied to cases of sexual abuse and molestation. In 1974 the United States created a National Center on Child Abuse and Neglect.

Child & Domestic Abuse

Since the 1970s, conservative and feminist groups have sought, for different reasons, aggressive measures to combat child abuse. Although earlier campaigns against child molestation had emphasized the threat posed by strangers, feminists stressed what they perceived as the vastly greater danger posed by male intimates, such as fathers, stepfathers, uncles, and brothers. Because abuse by male relatives is rarely reported by the family involved, child-welfare advocates called for new laws that would allow greater intervention by outside professionals. During the 1970s and '80s, most states adopted some form of mandatory reporting procedure whereby doctors, teachers, and social workers were required to report any circumstances that might reveal suspected child abuse. The courts also revamped their procedures to grant more protection to victims. For example, to remove the need for child witnesses to confront the accused, children often were permitted to testify from behind screens or even by video link from another room, and judges and lawyers were encouraged to frame questions and language in a way that did not baffle or intimidate children.

Along with the changes in laws and attitudes came a dramatic upsurge in the number of reported abuse cases. Between 1976 and 1986, reports of child abuse and neglect across the United States rose threefold to over two million, with a further increase to nearly three million reports by the mid-1990s. However, a majority of these reports were judged to be unfounded. Reports of sexual abuse rose 18-fold between 1976 and 1985. The increases in recorded child-abuse figures, which may have been a result of greater awareness of the problem rather than a surge in abuse, contributed to a widespread impression that society was suffering an "epidemic" of child abuse, and concern reached immense proportions during the 1980s.

Dr. Steven Gold (Psychotherapy Winter 1997 34:4 page 365) In a remarkably brief number of years the mental health professions have undergone several dramatic and surprisingly abrupt transformations in their position on childhood sexual abuse (CSA) and its effect on adjustment in adulthood. It is only as recently as the late 1970s and early 1980s that the scope and enduring adverse impact of child abuse came to be widely recognized in the professional and research literature (Browne & Finkelhor, 1986; Courtois, 1988; Meiselman, 1978). By the late 1980s and early 1990s, child abuse had become the focus of intense interest among both mental health professionals and the popular media. Just a few years later, in the mid-to-late 1990s, the prevalence, traumatic impact, and delayed recall of child abuse in general and

Introduction

child sexual abuse in particular were "hot topics," but also frequently sources of vehement debate and controversy (see, e.g., Loftus, 1993; Pope, 1996).

Dr. Christine A. Courtois & Dr. Steven N. Gold (Psychological Trauma 2009 1:1 page 3). For several decades now, the knowledge base about psychological trauma has been continually expanding in the professional literature (Friedman, Keane, & Resick, 2007). In the earliest days of the practice of psychotherapy in Europe in the late 19th century, trauma was recognized as playing an important role in the genesis and exacerbation of many psychological difficulties; however, for various reasons, appreciation of the relevance of the experience of trauma to many psychological problems waned through much of the 20th century (Friedman, Resick, & Keane, 2007; Herman, 1992b; van der Kolk, 2007; Monson, Friedman, & LaBash, 2007). It was only in the 1970s that the focused attention on psychological trauma resumed. This trend was catalyzed largely by the difficulties exhibited by Vietnam War veterans and emerging awareness, via the feminist movement, of the alarming prevalence of rape, domestic violence, and all forms of childhood abuse. Renewed awareness of trauma in the 1970s culminated in the inclusion of the diagnosis of posttraumatic stress disorder (PTSD) and the dissociative disorders (DDs) in the *DSM–III* in 1980 (American Psychiatric Association [APA], 1980). Since that time empirical and clinical exploration of psychological trauma has sustained and flourished. The extensive literature that has accumulated since the 1970s has simultaneously been accompanied by burgeoning awareness on a societal level of the broad reach, financial costs, and lasting adverse impact of traumatic events. In the final two decades of the 20th century, increasing sensitivity arose about the widespread and emotionally damaging nature of domestic violence, childhood abuse, and sexual assault...

Definition of abuse has been expanding recently

Originally the concept of abuse meant that a child was raped or severely beaten or touched in an obvious sexual manner. In recent years the term sexual abuse has been expanded to mean the use of a child for sexual arousal which might result from explicit touching or fondling or even hugging or having a child sit on his lap. The child is considered abused even if he is not aware of the sexual arousal of the perpetrator and is not necessarily disturbed by it. Similarly physical abuse is no longer

Child & Domestic Abuse

just a severe beating but could include slapping a child or giving him a spanking – something which was considered normal just a few years ago.

Encyclopedia Britannica (Child Abuse 2008). The legal definition of child abuse differs between societies and has changed significantly over time. For example, the age of sexual consent varies greatly between and even within countries. Some European countries prohibit the use of physical violence to enforce discipline, though others permit moderate forms of coercion. Despite these differences, the abusive treatment of children, however it is defined, is widely proscribed by criminal statutes. One of the earliest national laws to protect children from cruel treatment was adopted in Great Britain in 1884, when the National Society for the Prevention of Cruelty to Children was organized. Similar organizations subsequently were created in other countries. In the United States in 1875, New York became the first state to legislate protection for children. Its laws served as a model for other states, all of which developed statutes designating child abuse a criminal offense. In the 1880s American states systematically began raising the age at which girls could give sexual consent from 10, which had been in place since colonial times.

Beginning concern for children's welfare in society – 1870's

American Humane (Protecting Children & Animal since 1877): The sufferings of the little girl, Mary Ellen, led to the founding of the New York Society for the Prevention of Cruelty to Children, the first organization of its kind, in 1874. In 1877, the New York SPCC and several Societies for the Prevention of Cruelty to Animals from throughout the country joined together to form the American Humane Association. Mary Ellen's story marked the beginning of a world-wide crusade to save children. Over the years, in the re-telling of Mary Ellen Wilson's story, myth has often been confused with fact. Some of the inaccuracies stem from colorful but erroneous journalism, others from simple misunderstanding of the facts, and still others from the complex history of the child protection movement in the United States and Great Britain and its link to the animal welfare movement. While it is true that Henry Bergh, president of the American Society of the Prevention of Cruelty to Animals (ASPCA), was instrumental in ensuring Mary Ellen's removal from an abusive home, it is not true that her attorney—who also worked for the ASPCA—argued that she deserved help because she was "a member of the animal kingdom."

Introduction

Earliest responsa of child abuse are from 1850's

Tzemach Tzedek (237): Question: Concerning the suspect - the rav and posek of the teachers - who was playing with a boy on Purim and stuck his hands into the pants of the youth. The rabbi claimed that he did so because he is childless because he is impotent. He thought that this might be due to his small testicles and he wanted to know if his testicles were in fact smaller than normal. In other words, the rabbi claimed that he was conducting a medical examination on the boy. **Answer:** The Beis Yosef cites a Yerushalmi at the end of Simon 334 and the Kesef Mishna states in Chapter 7 of Hilchos Talmud Torah that a scholar who becomes bad is not to be removed from his position of honor. Therefore according to this when the gemora (Mo'ed Koton 17a) states that a Torah scholar who has become corrupt is still to be honored but he is to be returned to his home - must mean that he is not to be removed from his position at all. Therefore we must say that the poskim rule like Reish Lakish who says that a talmid chachom that becomes corrupt is not to be placed in nidoi (ostracized) and they rule also like R' Yehuda who banned a talmid chachom about whom there were constant bad rumors. Both of these issues are mentioned in Mo'ed Koton (17a)....

Sho'el U'Meishiv (1:185): Rumors spread about a certain teacher who had lived in that city for 8 years. Children that he had taught while they were young and now were 13 years or more testified that he had sodomized them when they were younger. The previous summer a certain G-d fearing man found out about this and was outraged and informed the rav of the community. However the rav did not want to accept this testimony. The teacher accepted on himself that after the semester was over he would leave the community. Later he decided he wanted to be a teacher in Lvov but when the people there heard rumors about this matter a respected layman sent a letter to the rav of the original community. The rav responded that he and his beis din investigated the matter and they found absolutely no basis that would invalidate the teacher according to the laws of the Torah. The rav added that the matter was not clarified but that a judge can only make decisions based on what he sees... Therefore he was hired as a teacher in Lvov...Now in the week of Parshas Va'era a letter came to me with the testimony signed by three respected men and one man who recognizes the signatures. Two men testified – one who is now 15 years old and one who is today older than 13 that in their youth when they learned with him when they were around 9 years or less he would sodomize them when they slept with

Child & Domestic Abuse

him in a single bed in the room where he lived. There were additional details that are too disgusting to put in this book...

Change results from knowledge of the harm of abuse

When trying to persuade the rabbis or community leaders to fight abuse - focusing on legalities as to what exactly was the sin transgressed is not helpful. It is also a waste of time discussing whether calling the police constitutes the sin of mesira or whether a rabbi has the power to impose a punishment in these cases. It is largely a waste of time arguing whether going to a secular court is permissible when they use the non-Torah punishment of prison. All these halachic considerations have legitimate authorities for both permitting and prohibiting a particular action. Typically existence of conflicting authorities leads to a stalemate. However the Rashba (3:393) states, "If we insist on doing only what is specified by Torah and not to punish except as specified in the Torah – the world will be destroyed."

A much more productive approach - and the only one that actually works in a tradition-oriented society - is to demonstrate that severe harm results from abuse. To the degree that the rabbis and community leaders can be convinced that abused children suffer horrible lifetime wounds, you will discover that the legal objections disappear. Pointing out to yeshivos and camp directors the fact that they are liable to multimillion dollar lawsuits for failing to protect children or that there is a long jail term for covering up or ignoring this abuse - is a much more convincing argument to increase protection for children. The publicity and resulting chilul hashem from newspaper articles and Internet discussions puts tremendous pressure on the community to stop abuse. The publicizing of arrests and jail sentences of abusers also convinces people that the problem is not a few deviates but that the problem involves our friends, family and leaders. Finally it is important to know that if we as parents, professionals and community members empathically and repeatedly say that abuse is intolerable – the views of the leaders will follow.

Betrayal by family & authorities is also abuse

One of the major issues frequently mentioned by the victims of abuse and their families is that they not only suffer from abuse but equally harmful - they feel betrayed. Rabbis and community leaders are expected to provide protection against harm. Even if harm is done, they are expected to make efforts to take measures so that it doesn't happen again and to help the victim recover. This unfortunately is not

Introduction

always the case and in fact it is not unusual that the complaining victim is viewed as the troublemaker and not the abuser.

For example, a rabbinic judge who deals with these cases told me that there was a case of a father who was raping his teen-age daughter. The mother came to him and asked him for permission to go to the police – which he granted. However as the result of their reporting the incident, the family was driven out of their community in New York and is now living in Israel. They were betrayed by their community.

It is fairly common that when a child finally gets the courage to report that a family member or teacher is abusing him, he is severely criticized and punished by his parents or school for slandering an "innocent person." Instead of being comforted and protected, the victim is abused again by the betrayal and is left unprotected from his molester.

Actually it is not only the victim and his family who feel betrayed. I was approached one Shabbos by a friend who had heard that I was working on this book and wanted to know if I was aware that "X" was a child molester. "X" happened to be a well-known and respected member of our community and I had not heard he was a molester. My friend is a frum child therapist in the neighborhood and is well placed to be up to date on these matters. He said he was shocked to learn "X", who was one of his neighbors, had a history of molesting children going back at least 10 years. ["X" was arrested and convicted of child molestation when two teenagers reported him to the police two weeks later – with the encouragement of a community rabbi]. When my friend asked some of the local rabbis why the community wasn't warned he was told simply – "but everyone knew about it." Obviously not every one knew about it and as is fairly common – none of the parents of molested boys wanted to press charges. My friend who is an FFB – expressed anger and hurt that the system had not taken elementary measures to protect others including his children from harm.

Major paradigm shift in Orthodox community

Over the last few years a major shift in how abuse is viewed is occurring - not only in the secular world - but also the Orthodox world. Rabbis, communities, parents and schools are beginning to look at abuse as a reality that must be dealt with. Originally abuse was viewed as an unusual occurrence that represented a moral lapse of the abuser and only caused discomfort to the victim. Common wisdom was that it was best dealt with by cover-ups or simply ignoring complaints. Just as in the secular

Child & Domestic Abuse

world, the injury and trauma of abuse is now being considered a real and pervasive issue, so too is it becoming viewed in the Orthodox world. Of course the degree that this shift of understanding has penetrated our communities varies widely. The indicator of this change is evidenced by the degree to which abuse is reacted to by legalistic terms such as, "Where are the witnesses?, "What was the nature of the accusations?", Who is the accused perpetrator?" or "Who knows about it?" In contrast where the shift has occurred the same facts are reacted to by a different set of questions i.e., How can we help the victim and prevent future pain?"

It is not an indication of how religiously observant the community or rabbi is – but rather the degree to which the price of ignoring abuse is known. Those who are aware of the nature of the psychological damage, the bad publicity, lawsuits and prison sentences awaiting the perpetrators – react with a much greater concern for the victim. Those who are unaware of these serious consequences of abuse or don't want to know - are more likely to be focused on the impact on the community, school or family if the issue isn't covered up or the community or school takes care of the matter.

Another major factor in the changing attitude towards abuse – is the fact that the children and grandchildren of rabbis also get abused. Those who have seen first hand what abuse does to a beloved child become much more sensitive to the issue.

Shameful to talk about abuse - but so is denying it

The topic of this book presents a dilemma. On the one hand it is disgusting and embarrassing to publicly discuss this issue – especially for an audience which is very careful to avoid explicit mention about such matters. Furthermore it is demeaning and disgraceful to publicize that such behavior happens within our community. There is also the issue of chilul Hashem. This is the fundamental principle in Judaism that any negative information publicized about Jews reflects badly on G-d's presence in this world. On the other hand, the problem unfortunately exists and that not talking about it and repressing awareness of these crimes is causing much greater permanent harm. Moreover it is clear that the negative consequences of not trying to stop this horrible problem - as well as the disgrace and shame that results from attempts to cover-up and deny the problem - are clearly a greater chilul Hashem then the abuse itself.

Yoma (86a): What is chilul Hashem? … R' Nachman bar Yitzchok said chilul Hashem results when a person studies Bible, learns Mishna and has intensive interaction with talmidei chachom but is not honest in business and doesn't have a

Introduction

pleasant way of talking with people – people say, "Woe is the person who studies Torah, woe is his father who taught him Torah, woe is his teacher who taught him Torah because this man studies Torah and look how disgusting his deeds are and how ugly are his ways!…

Child & Domestic Abuse

Mayo Clinic Report on Pedophilia (2007)

Effects of abuse on children

(page 465) Generally, abused children experience the greatest psychological damage when the abuse occurs from father figures (close neighbors, priests or ministers, coaches) or involves force and/or genital contact.[5,45,46] The specific long-term effects on abused children as they grow into adulthood are difficult to predict. Some individuals adapt and have a higher degree of resilience, whereas others are profoundly and negatively changed. Studies have found that the children abused by pedophiles have higher measures of trauma, depression, and neurosis on standardized psychometric testing.[45,46] Individuals who experience long-term abuse are significantly more likely to have affective illness (eg, depression), anxiety disorders (eg, generalized anxiety disorders, posttraumatic stress disorder, panic attacks), eating disorders (anorexia in females), substance abuse, personality disorders, and/or adjustment disorders and to make suicidal gestures or actually engage in serious suicide attempts than those who are not abused. These children often have problems with long-term intimacy and feelings of guilt and shame over their role in the incident.

Number of victims per molester & amount of abuse

(Page 459) A study by Abel et al [32] of 377 nonincarcerated, non–incest-related pedophiles, whose legal situations had been resolved and who were surveyed using an anonymous self-report questionnaire, found that heterosexual pedophiles on average reported abusing 19.8 children and committing 23.2 acts, whereas homosexual pedophiles had abused 150.2 children and committed 281.7 acts. These studies confirm law enforcement reports about the serial nature of the crime, the large number of children abused by each pedophile, and the underreporting of assaults.

Treatment

(Page 465) No treatment for pedophilia is effective unless the pedophile is willing to engage in the treatment. Individuals can offend again while in active psychotherapy,

Mayo Clinic Report on Pedophilia (2007)

while receiving pharmacologic treatment, and even after castration.[17] Currently, much of the focus of pedophilic treatment is on stopping further offenses against children rather than altering the pedophile's sexual orientation toward children. Schober et al[34] found that individuals still showed sexual interest in children, as measured by the AASI, even after a year of combined psychotherapy and pharmacotherapy, whereas the pedophiles' self-reported frequency of urges and masturbation had decreased. These findings indicate that the urges can be managed, but the core attraction does not change. Other interventions designed to manage these pedophilic urges include careful forensic and therapeutic monitoring and reporting, use of testosterone-lowering medications, use of SSRIs, and surgical castration.

(Page 466) Psychotherapy is an important aspect of treatment, although debate exists concerning its overall effectiveness for long-term prevention of new offenses.[47,91-93] Psychotherapy can be individual, group based, or, most commonly, a combination of the two. The general strategy toward psychotherapy with pedophiles is a cognitive behavioral approach (addressing their distortions and denial) combined with empathy training, sexual impulse control training, relapse prevention, and biofeedback. Several studies have demonstrated that the best outcomes in preventing repeat offenses against children occur when pharmacological agents and psychotherapy are used together.

Recidivism Rate

(Page 467) Just as the prevalence of pedophilia is not accurately known, the rate of recidivism against a child is also unknown. Recidivism is a term with many definitions, which affect reported rates of repeated offenses. For example, some studies look at additional arrests for any offense, others only look at arrests for sexual crimes, and some only look at convictions, whereas others analyze self-reported reoffenses.[31,94,96] The data on recidivism underestimate its rate because many treatment studies do not include treatment dropout figures, cannot calculate the number of repeated offenses that are not reported, and do not use polygraphs to confirm self-reports.[96] Another complicating factor is the period during which the data are collected. Some studies report low recidivism rates, but these numbers apply to individuals followed up during periods of active treatment only or for short periods after treatment is terminated (eg, 1-5 years). The published rates of recidivism are in the range of 10% to 50% for pedophiles depending on their grouping.

Child & Domestic Abuse

(Page 467) Most of the repeated offenses occurred 10 years after the initial offense. Whether this delay was initially due to successful treatment, incarceration, or other factors is unknown. Beier KM. Differential typology and prognosis for dissexual behavior—a follow-up study of previously expert-appraised child molesters. *Int J Legal Med.* 1998;111:133-141.]

Complete report is available on Mayo Clinic Website.

http://www.mayoclinicproceedings.com/content/82/4/457.full

*Two halachic frameworks – defensive vs. judicial

By Rav Yehuda Silman

Rav Yehuda Silman (Yeschurun 22): Question: I had previously received a query from America concerning the issue of informing the government authorities in a case of a teacher sexually abusing his student. The question was whether it is permitted or even a mitzva to be involved in reporting the matter to the secular authorities. I replied [Yeschurun 15 page 661] that there are number of different ways to judge the matter. 1) **Viewing the abuser as a rodef** (pursuer) [I mentioned in the previous article that this does not apply in the case of a male above the age of 13 or a girl above the age of 12 when the adult does it with their consent.]. 2) **Stopping the abuser from sinning**. I brought the dispute between the Ketzos and the Nesivos HaMishpat…and the Yam Shel Shlomo and the Chasam Sofer. However it is agreed by all of these sources is that a person of distinguished status (chashiv) is able to stop another from committing a prohibited act. 3) **The position of Shulchan Aruch (C.M. 2)** that a beis din is able to flog and punish in order to protect society – in a manner which is not prescribed by the Torah. Therefore in a case like ours in which experience has shown that a sex abuser is able to ruin many people – everyone agrees that beis din can punish in ways not prescribed by the Torah. [In the earlier article I pointed out there are significant differences between these approaches. If you take the perspective of separating the abuser from sinning then if the teacher is fired then there is no longer a need to act since he has lost his primary opportunity to sin but of course it depends on the nature of the crime. In contrast if the concern is protecting society then the perpetrator should still be reported even if he has been fired.] 4) **The view expressed in Bava Metzia (83b)** concerning R' Eliezar bar Rav Shimon who was involved in capturing thieves because the king had commanded him to do so. I brought the dispute amongst the rishonim was to whether or not the halacha is in accord with R' Eliezar or not. In the original article I was inclined to the view that in the case of sexual abuse since the perpetrator is not executed but is imprisoned to

Child & Domestic Abuse

protect society then perhaps all would agree that it is permitted to report him to the authorities.

Furthermore in the original article it was concluded that it is obvious that there is no need to have witnesses that meet the standards required by the Torah but even less than that is sufficient and I cited a number of rishonim. The reason is reporting the teacher to the secular authorities is not punishment requiring a beis din but is an action mandated by secular law (in the Diaspora) or in order to separate the abuser from committing sin. In addition according to the reason that even in the case of a possible rodef it is permitted to inform the authorities – it is obvious that is permitted without proper witnesses since all that is required is that there be the possibility that he is an abuser.

... In fact these cases do not require a beis din and we need to merely consider the possible loss versus the possible gain. If the accusations are in fact true then we are dealing with a case of saving a person from being harmed. While if the accusations are in fact not true then in general then the government will free him. On the other hand it is certain that it is impossible that everyone can take responsibility for deciding whether to inform the secular authorities. That is because the majority of people do not have the prerequisite Torah knowledge or professional knowledge to establish whether the evidence is serious and the concern is genuine. Thus of necessity these matters should only be dealt with by an established beis din or at least an experience rabbi who has had a lot of experience dealing with cases of abuse. It is also clear that the beis din or the rav needs to make the decision only after appropriate consultation with professionals. ..."

Guidelines of Orthodox Organizations

Association of Jewish Camp Operators - 2006

MEIR FRISCHMAN *Director* 23 Sivan, 5766 June 19, 2006

Dear Director/Operator:

As you are aware, over the years AJCO has issued guidelines and advisory suggestions relating to important safety issues for our campers and staff members. (A case in point - the Driving Guidelines.) In addition, a number of years ago, we sponsored a forum which discussed issues pertaining to the painful subject of child molestation and abuse. Now, as the new camp season is about to begin, let me take this opportunity to communicate with you on this subject once again.

It is obvious that the overwhelming majority of our campers enjoy healthy and happy summer experiences. Boruch Hashem, to the best of our knowledge, any allegations of inappropriate conduct have been few and far between. However, in order to ensure the highest levels of safety, we must be constantly vigilant and take appropriate steps to sensitize parents, campers and staff to help avoid any potential problems; and to have a procedure in place if chas v'shalom any problem does arise.

Accordingly, I am enclosing for your consideration two documents. The first is a suggested text of a pre-camp mailing to parents, including a cover letter encouraging parents to speak to their children about the importance of maintaining the privacy and integrity of their bodies, and a "Keep it Safe" fact sheet with specific suggestions of what parents should tell their children. These documents were prepared at the recommendation of the Moetzes Gedolei HaTorah of Agudath Israel of America, whose members feel that parents should indeed be encouraged to speak to their children about these matters. In developing the suggested points to be relayed by parents to children, we had the benefit of input by the renowned professional staff at Ohel Children's Home and Family Services, who have considerable expertise in these matters, and who have informed us that they stand ready to help in any way including

Child & Domestic Abuse

providing staff training, consultations to camp directors, evaluation and treatment whenever deemed appropriate.

The second document is a page from the staff handbook that we at Camp Agudah distribute to our staff members, in order to provide them with guidance on appropriate behavior as well as other pertinent matters. This document is modeled on the guidelines issued by Torah Umesorah and approved and adopted by our senior Roshei Yeshiva and Rabbonim for implementation in the yeshivos.

We encourage you to include this topic in any pre-summer orientation sessions you have with staff. Again, drawing on Camp Agudah's experience, over the past several years we have had a knowledgeable mental health professional speak to our staff on this subject before the summer. This has proven to be an effective means of sensitizing them to the issue, above and beyond the written guidance provided in the handbook.

Several camps with which we have been in contact have told us that they plan to make a mailing to their parents and train their staff, as Camp Agudah is doing. In my opinion, and in the view of the Gedolei Yisroel with whom we have discussed the matter, a pro-active approach by all Jewish camp administrations on this issue is both appropriate and necessary in today's day and age. I believe this will be very much appreciated by all of our parent bodies.

Finally, although it goes without saying, the ultimate achrayus of dealing with any individual situation of alleged improper conduct rests with us as camp directors. It is therefore incumbent upon us to carefully review the circumstances surrounding any claim of improper conduct, and to determine the appropriate course of action. Such action may even require reporting to the civil authorities in certain situations. We recommend that each camp should work with a competent attorney, mental health professional, and of course its moreh hora'ah in following through on any given situation that may arise.

Best wishes for a successful summer camp season, with only besoros tovos to share amongst one another.

Guidelines of Orthodox Organizations

Suggested cover letter to parents

Dear Parents:

We respectfully take the liberty of communicating with you about an extremely important issue that deserves your personal consideration as we get ready for what will b'ezras Hashem be a wonderful camp season.

Over the years, The Association of Jewish Camp Operators (AJCO), which serves as an umbrella group for Orthodox Jewish summer camps, has issued guidelines and suggestions at the request of our Gedolei Rabbonim and Roshei Yeshiva on a number of issues, such as the Safe Driving Guidelines in the Mountains.

In response to inquiries from a number of camps, the Moetzes Gedolei HaTorah of Agudath Israel of America recently discussed the sensitive topic of protecting the privacy and bodily integrity of our children. Among other things, they encouraged the summer camps to take positive steps to help avoid any potential problems - including enlisting parents to discuss this subject with their children before sending them off to camp. They further requested that AJCO prepare a document guiding parents on how to advise their children to respond in the event their bodily privacy has been threatened or cbas t/shalom violated. This is particularly important in light of the fact that children generally do not self-disclose they were inappropriately touched or abused and at times may not realize or understand they are being abused.

Accordingly, we are enclosing a "Keep it Safe" fact sheet that has been prepared by AJCO in conjunction with the experts at OHEL Children's Home and Family Services. We respectfully urge you to speak to your child or children and convey to them the important points outlined in the enclosed document.

As a member of AJCO, and understanding the importance of this issue, we are committed to taking every step in our power to protect the safety of our campers and staff. We will be doing our part by sensitizing staff regarding this issue, and we respectfully enlist your assistance in speaking to your children as well. Of course, please feel free to call us if any issue or problem arises, or if you have any further questions.

Looking forward to a wonderful summer, both b'ruchniyus uvegashmius.

Child & Domestic Abuse

Things to Tell Your Child Before the Camp Season

Explain to your child that there are unfortunately a small number of people with a sickness that gives them a yetzer hara to touch children immodestly -. i.e. in a place ordinarily covered by a bathing suit.

Teach your child that no one, not even a person in a position of authority or a close relative, has the right to touch him or her in such a way.

Teach your child that it is OK to say to such a person, "No, get away." Let your child know that he should tell you or a trusted member of the camp administration, such as the camp director or head counselor, about any inappropriate touching. Emphasize that this does not constitute loshon hora or any other aveirah; and that in fact it is a mitzvah to report such matters.

Tell your child that he should not listen to anyone who tells them to "keep secrets" from his parents or from the camp administration.

Tell your child that he should not be afraid of threats from anyone who touches him improperly. Both you and the camp administration will protect him.

GENERAL POINTERS

Be alert for changes in your child's behavior that could signal abuse, such as sudden secretiveness, sleeplessness, and withdrawal from activities or increased anxiety.

If your child is a victim of abuse, don't blame him. Listen and consult with a competent professional.

Above all, let your child know that he can always tell you anything without fear of blame

Communication is critical.

Guidelines of Orthodox Organizations

Behavioral Standards of Camp Aguda

We would like to address the issue/problem of child molestation & abuse.

In the past, a small number of individuals have caused untold pain to a large number of children primarily varying in ages from three to fourteen. In addition to the sins which they have committed, they have created painful memories in the minds of their victims, memories which can have a devastating lifetime impact. The Rabbinical Board of Torah Umesorab has issued a set of behavioral and reporting standards /or principals to implement in their yeshivos and day schools, which, it is hoped, will strengthen the protection of students. We, at camp, have developed the following behavioral standards which are modeled on the Torah Umesorah guidelines. -reprinted with permission from the Camp Agudah staff handbook

While the overwhelming majority of interactions amongst staff and students fall well within the range of normal healthy relationships, certain behaviors are incompatible with the goals and standards of a camp and Jewish upbringing and, therefore, are always prohibited. Violation of these standards is grounds for immediate dismissal or other appropriate disciplinary action.

- Counselors/staff may not be alone with a child/children in a locked room or in any area that cannot be seen or observed by other faculty members or adults. Staff members should not be in campers' bunks that are not their own, especially at night.

- Counselors/staff should avoid all unnecessary physical contact with campers, especially any which can be interpreted as being of a sexually motivated or physically abusive nature, such as inappropriate touching or excessive "rough-housing". For example, a camper should not sit on a staff member's lap. Nor should a staff member touch a camper while he is sleeping.

- Counselors/staff may never forbid campers from sharing any conversations or information with parents or administration, nor instruct students to "keep secrets" from their parents or administration officials.

- Counselors/staff must refrain from any immodest behavior or speech and from inappropriate jokes or innuendoes.

Child & Domestic Abuse

_ Any explicit or indirect invitation to engage in inappropriate or suggestive activities, which mayor may not include a promise of reward for complying, or a threat of reprisal for not complying, constitute a violation of camp policy and should be immediately reported to the Director or Head Counselor.

Where any staff member has reason to believe a violation of any of the above rules has occurred, he should report it immediately to Director or Head Counselor.

The reporting of fondling, inappropriate touching, or any form of lewdness to the Director or Head Counselor does not constitute loshon hora or any other *aveirah*. On the contrary, *Gedolei Yisroel* have ruled that such reporting is required by *halacha*.

Guidelines of Orthodox Organizations

Vaad harabbonim of Baltimore 2007

(The following letter was mailed to the members of Baltimore's Orthodox Community on April 11 from the Vaad Harabbonim, the Rabbinical Council of Greater Baltimore.)

There is no subject more painful for us to discuss than the issue of sexual abuse within our community. Yet at this point we believe it is the subject most necessary to address. We must acknowledge that this horrible form of abuse exists – and has existed for generations – in our community as well. This issue must be confronted directly and we believe that this discussion can be a first step towards the necessary and achievable goal of ridding our community of this scourge.

We feel it essential to discuss the matter directly with you, as the greatest allies of the abuser are ignorance and silence. The abuser preys on people who cannot understand that what he is doing to them is so very wrong. And the abuser thrives in an environment where he is confident that his victims will not report what they have experienced or where their reports of abuse will not be taken seriously. We therefore urge you to discuss this matter in a sensitive and non-alarming manner with your children so that they will clearly understand that they should forcefully refuse and immediately report inappropriate touch. They need to know that should, Heaven forbid, something like this ever occur to them, they will have somewhere to turn. And if they turn to you, you must respond compassionately, deliberately and with competent rabbinic and/or professional guidance, understanding that the thoughtful measure of your response will have enormous impact on your child's future.

We feel additionally compelled to discuss this issue openly in order to assist – in some small way – in the healing of survivors. Abuse often creates terrible confusion in the minds of its victims who may not understand the terrible wrong they have experienced, or who may blame themselves for the abuse. Addressing the issue clearly and definitively allows survivors of abuse to see that our contempt is reserve for those violated them, whereas they – the survivors – are so richly deserving of our compassion and our respect.

We cannot speak with certainty to the prevalence of abuse in our community. It is clear however that any single abuser will often have many victims. Those who abuse within the family – and this horror absolutely does happen – often victimize numerous

Child & Domestic Abuse

family members. A coach, camp counselor, teacher, principal or rabbi who abuses his charges throughout his career has had the opportunity to abuse hundreds of children. We can say without question that across the nation we have had prolific abusers in these positions, and consequently, we have hundreds of survivors in our communities.

The damage that abuse can cause is devastating and potentially life altering: it commonly ruins an individual's sense of self, their ability to trust others, and their ability to engage in a healthy intimate relationship. Furthermore, there is a growing consensus amongst mental health professionals serving the observant community that many of our "teens-at-risk" issues were generated by incidents of abuse. The risks of suicide, alcohol and drug abuse and other self-destructive behaviors are all increased dramatically by abuse.

As such it is already well established by our own Poskim that an abuser is to be considered a Rodef (literally a "pursuer"), effectively poised to destroy innocent lives and, therefore, virtually all means may be used to stop him and bring him to justice. Communities and day schools – with the blessing of Gedolei Yisroel – have encouraged and facilitated the reporting of these crimes to the local authorities, who are most equipped to investigate and prosecute these complex claims.

In the past, many mistakes were made in handling these situations. Abusers were often not recognized for what they were, as it was too difficult to believe that otherwise good people could do such things, nor was it sufficiently appreciated what damage such acts could cause. It was often thought that if the abuser was spoken to or warned, and perhaps moved to a different environment, he would never do these things again. In responding this way many terrible mistakes were made and tragic consequences resulted. We have seen too often the immediate or eventual failure of these "behind-the-scenes agreements" to keep the perpetrators away from others. Naiveté and a lack of understanding of the insidious nature of these perpetrators have allowed the toll of victims to rise. These failures haunt us – but they also motivate us to respond more effectively and wisely in the future.

An abuser is not simply a lustful person, plagued by a Taavah – a desire – that can be addressed with sincere Teshuva. He has a severe illness, that may be incurable, and that is at best enormously difficult to manage. Publicizing his status as an abuser – while causing enormous damage to his own family – may be the only way to truly protect the community from him.

Guidelines of Orthodox Organizations

Can we produce the same result – safety for the community – without going public? We do not know if we can. We do know that we as rabbis are not qualified to manage the behavior of such a person such that we can confidently say that he poses no threat to his community. Understanding, treating and managing this illness is a highly complex field that we are not properly trained in. There are specialized professionals in this area whose experience and expertise we must call upon to guide us.

They – as experts in this most complex field – may consider specific situations to be safely manageable using a professionally designed – and consistently and vigilantly guided – protocol for the individual abuser. But in many cases the most effective method to protect the community will be in publicizing the abuser's identity. In all situations we must be mindful that our obligation to protect future potential victims of sexual abuse is paramount.

A final word about false accusation: We are very sensitive about the possibility of false accusations which, themselves, cause enormous pain and damage. This obliges us, therefore, to ensure at the outset that claims and counterclaims are investigated objectively and fairly by those most trained and equipped to do so.

The issues discussed here are most complex and very painful. But they must be discussed and this problem must be addressed.

Allow us to summarize with a few action points.

1. We must educate our children about inappropriate touch, so that they will clearly understand that they should forcefully refuse and immediately report inappropriate touch.

2. Credible concerns of abuse must be reported to the authorities who have expertise, experience and wisdom to thoroughly and responsibly investigate them. We as Rabbanim are committed to facilitating and supporting this process.

3. We must have, and we are in the process of developing, a clear approach to protecting our community, both here and elsewhere, from established or strongly suspected abusers. This approach could possibly include a professionally designed, and consistently and vigilantly guided, management protocol for the individual. Many situations will require the drastic step of publicizing the identity and the dangers posed by the perpetrator.

Child & Domestic Abuse

Effective action can really go a long way. If we can begin to approach this issue wisely and confidently we can create a climate where abuse would rarely occur and where, if it does happen, it would always be addressed promptly.

We pray that Hashem spare us such tragedies in the future, and that He grant us the wisdom and the courage to responsibly address the threats we currently face.

Guidelines of Orthodox Organizations

Rabbinical Council of America - 2010

Apr 27, 2010 -- Whereas we have become increasingly aware of incidents of the sexual and physical abuse of children in our community; and

Whereas, there have been a number of high profile cases in which Orthodox rabbis have been indicted or convicted for child abuse or child endangerment; and

Whereas the lives and futures of many of these victims and their families are harmed in significant ways: suicide, post traumatic stress syndrome, inability to form healthy relationships, inability to develop healthy intimate relationships, etc.; and

Whereas many victims of abuse in our community still remain silent and do not come forward to accuse perpetrators or seek help for fear of stigma, personal and familial consequences, or perceived halakhic concerns; and

Whereas the Rabbinical Council of America has resolved through past resolutions its condemnation of abuse and its censure of abusers, and has affirmed, under the guidance and direction of its poskim (Rabbinic decisors,) that the prohibitions of mesirah (reporting crimes to the civil authorities) and arka'ot (adjudication in civil courts) do not apply in cases of abuse and in fact, it is halakhically obligatory to make such reports; and

Whereas reiterating this long held position can serve to provide pastoral and halakhic leadership, support, direction and affirmation to abuse survivors and their families and advocates.

Therefore, the Rabbinical Council of America resolves that

- It reaffirms its unqualified condemnation of all forms of child abuse.
- It reaffirms its halakhic position that the prohibitions of mesirah and arka'ot do not apply in cases of abuse.
- It will regularly issue on its website and to the media appropriate statements of condemnation when public attention is drawn to a case in which Jews are either victims or perpetrators of abuse.

Child & Domestic Abuse

- It will regularly evaluate the competence of its members in understanding and responding to issues of child abuse and initiate training and continuing educational opportunities for all of its members in this area every year.

- The members of the RCA address the issues of child abuse in their communities in at least one sermon, lecture or article within the next twelve months, and that contact information for local abuse services be displayed in a public place in all synagogues, schools, and Jewish community institutions serviced by its members.

Guidelines of Orthodox Organizations

Agudath Israel & Torah U'Mesorah

Fingerprinting

Rabbi David Zweibel executive vice president of Agudath Israel of America (**Jewish Star** November 12, 2008):

"We'd be happier if there was some experience [with the voluntary bill]," Zweibel said, "but it's not worth allowing our position to be distorted as being in some ways not supportive of finger printing."

"Fingerprinting happens to be a tool among a larger array of things that need to be done and frankly it's not the most powerful tool." Zwiebel continued. "It's being used by the rest of society and there's good reason why we ought to use the tool for whatever it's worth."

Abuse and blogs

Rabbi David Zweibel executive vice president of Agudath Israel of America (**Jewish Star** November 12, 2008):

"[Sexual abuse] is an issue which has come out of the closet in a certain sense and is engaging the attention of our community and its leadership and that's ultimately a good thing. That's why it's hard for me to be totally annoyed with some of the excesses of the blog world. Their outrage, anger, and sometimes excessive advocacy and negativity towards the establishment, it's a terrible thing, but at the same time, I know that their hearts are in the right place and it is stuff to be very upset about. Is Agudah a fair target? I think we could always use a healthy dose of introspection and honest assessment of how well we as a society have performed in this area and lots of other areas."

Government shouldn't seem to be taking power from rabbis

New York Times (October 14, 2009 Orthodox Jews Rely More on Sex Abuse Prosecution *By Paul Vitello):*

David Zwiebel, executive vice president of Agudath Israel of America, a group representing many chareidi factions, offered the moderate view. "A broad consensus has emerged in the last few years," he said, "that many of these issues are beyond the ability of the community to handle internally."

Child & Domestic Abuse

But he added that prosecutors should recognize "religious sensitivities" by seeking alternatives to prison, to avoid depriving a family of its breadwinner, or by finding appropriate Orthodox homes for children removed from abusive families.

"The district attorney should be careful not to be seen as making a power grab from rabbinic authority," Mr. Zwiebel said.

Severity of abuse problem was not known

Rabbi David Zweibel executive vice president of Agudath Israel of America **The Jewish Daily**, October 10, 2008

"Until not terribly long ago, the issue was very much in the shadows," said David Zwiebel, director of government affairs and general counsel of Agudath Israel of America. "The fact that there were isolated reports here and there of cases arising in yeshiva settings, it was known, but they were very isolated."

"Sometimes they were dealt with correctly and sometimes incorrectly," Zwiebel added, "but the severity of the problem and the possible magnitude were really things that most people, including myself, just didn't understand."

We can't allow lawsuits which could close yeshivos

New York (April 2009) - **Agudath Israel of America and Torah U'Mesorah** – The National Society for Hebrew Day Schools, upon consultation with their respective rabbinic leaderships, respectfully submit this statement regarding legislative proposals to amend existing statutes of limitations for civil claims, including claims against schools and other communal institutions, based on allegations of child sexual abuse. We do so only after much serious thought, after weighing all relevant arguments and for the sole purpose of protecting the most fundamental interests of our community.

Agudath Israel and Torah U'Mesorah fully acknowledge the horror of child sexual abuse and the devastating long-term scars it all too often creates. Our rabbinic and lay leaderships are acutely aware of the emotional trauma and damage caused by the perpetrators of such abuse. Our hearts go out to their victims, and we share in their pain. We realize that for too long many victims have suffered alone. We are committed as a community to do whatever we can to root out perpetrators of child abuse from our schools and other communal institutions, and to help victims on the road to healing and recovery.

Guidelines of Orthodox Organizations

Indeed, in recent years, as awareness has increased and sensitivity has been heightened regarding the incidence of sexual abuse and its severity, both in the broader society around us and in our community specifically, Agudath Israel and Torah U'Mesorah have taken a number of concrete steps to help ensure that Jewish schools, extra-curricular youth programs and summer camps implement policies and procedures designed to protect children against such abuse. Our organizations have also supported legislative efforts to furnish such protection, including the recently enacted legislation in New York authorizing nonpublic schools to screen all prospective employees through the state's fingerprint checking system.

With respect to the proposed amendments to existing statutes of limitations, Agudath Israel and Torah U'Mesorah fully understand that the trauma of abuse is often so great that young adults may not be emotionally prepared to file claims against their abusers within the traditional limitations period. Strict adherence to the existing statutes of limitations could thus operate to preclude certain legitimate claims and protect perpetrators of abuse. Our organizations would therefore have no objection to legislation designed to give victims of abuse greater recourse against perpetrators. Nor would we object to extending statutes of limitations for criminal proceedings against perpetrators.

What Agudath Israel and Torah U'Mesorah must object to, however, is legislation that could literally destroy schools, houses of worship that sponsor youth programs, summer camps and other institutions that are the very lifeblood of our community.

To take perhaps the most problematic example of such legislation, bills have been introduced in New York and other states that would create a one year window during which any civil claim based upon child sexual abuse could be brought, even against schools and other communal institutions, regardless of how long ago the incident is alleged to have taken place. One could envision a scenario in which a senior citizen might choose to bring a claim against a school for an incident that allegedly occurred over half-a-century ago when the claimant was a child. The fact that the alleged perpetrator may have passed on, or that the administration of the school may have changed several times since the alleged abuse, or that the school no longer has any records or insurance policies dating back to the time the abuse allegedly occurred, or even any records of the individual ever having attended the school, would be of no moment whatsoever under the proposed bill. The current school administration,

Child & Domestic Abuse

entirely ignorant of what may or may not have occurred so many years ago, would be forced to defend the school in a court of law, incur the high expenses of legal fees and diversion of human resources, and face potentially crippling financial liability.

It is important to recognize that Jewish schools are independent entities supported wholly by parental tuition and fundraising. Therefore, the burden of litigation expense or legal liability for ancient claims would fall squarely on an entirely innocent group – the current parent body. Needless to say, in today's perilous financial climate, as many parents are unable to meet even their basic tuition obligations and schools struggle to remain fiscally viable, this burden would be extremely difficult to bear, and could ultimately lead to school closures.

Stated simply, legislation that would do away with the statute of limitations completely, even if only for a one-year period, could subject schools and other vital institutions to ancient claims and capricious litigation, and place their very existence in severe jeopardy. Agudath Israel and Torah U'Mesorah most vigorously oppose any such legislation.

We must continue to seek out ways to protect our precious children and help eradicate molestation and other forms of abuse. We must also redouble our efforts to help those who have suffered the horrors of child abuse obtain the healing they so desperately need. However, we dare not bring down our most vital communal institutions in the process.

Guidelines of Orthodox Organizations

Ohel & Mandated Reporting

Statement Concerning Mandated Reporting

As with doctors and lawyers, the confidentiality relationship between a therapist and client can only be broken in extremely rare and prescribed circumstances.

Section 413 of NY State Social Services Law generally requires mandated reporters (therapists, teachers, social workers etc) to report suspected child abuse when they have reasonable cause to suspect that a parent, guardian or other person legally responsible for the child has abused and neglected the child.

Mental Hygiene Law Limited situations when therapist-client relationship can be broken as when there is an imminent risk to specifically identified person.

OHEL fully complies with New York state laws, including those related to mandated reporting. OHEL provides information and support to victims and parents, enabling them to report to the police instances of sexual abuse. OHEL cooperates with police and prosecutors in any investigation.

Child & Domestic Abuse

Flatbush Shomrim - 2010

The following important alert is from the **Flatbush Shomrim** April 2010.

Pedophiles Beware: The Flatbush Shomrim Safety Patrol continues to have a zero tolerance policy for pedophiles, predators and abusers. If you feel the need to abuse or behave inappropriately against someone, get help now. Therapy will help you. If you don't get help, you will be caught. When a call comes into our hotline we will respond and find you. In accordance with Daas Torah, you will be arrested and prosecuted.

Parents Beware: The summer months are approaching and our children will be out on the streets. Teach them to protect themselves from being touched improperly or spoken to inappropriately. An offender's work may take just minutes. The effect it leaves lasts a lifetime.

We would like to share the following safety tips BASED ON ACTUAL EVENTS. We've received complaints of abuse occurring in libraries, MTA buses, car services, parks, in the streets, etc.

- **Warn your children to never accept rides from strangers**. Children usually take the same route every day. They stand at the same bus stops, etc. They are vulnerable. Pedophiles know this and will wait patiently before making a move. A predator may have a beard and a yarmulke and may even be a family acquaintance.

- **Encourage your child to tell you about any unusual incidents**. For example, an adult acting too familiar or improperly or discussing inappropriate topics with them. Anywhere. Teach your children to be alert and to identify people by memorizing clothing description, car models, license plate numbers and other details of anyone looking suspicious.

- When at the park DO NOT send your child to the restroom alone. Pedophiles lurk around parks looking for easy targets.

- **NEVER send your children alone in a car service**. While most drivers are fine and hardworking people, we've had numerous complaints involving children and adults being victimized by predators working for car services.

Guidelines of Orthodox Organizations

Report all suspicious activity to the police first by calling 911. Then, call our 24 hour Emergency Hotline at 718-338-9797. If your call is of a sensitive nature please ask our dispatcher if you can speak with a coordinator. All calls will be kept confidential.

Child & Domestic Abuse

Torah u'Mesora: Behavioral standards for educators

While the overwhelming majority of interactions amongst staff and students fall well within the range of normal healthy relationships, certain behaviors are incompatible with the goals and standards of a yeshiva and Jewish upbringing and, therefore, are always prohibited.

- Teachers/staff may not be alone with a child/children in a locked room or in any area that cannot be seen or observed by other faculty members or adults.

- Teachers/staff must avoid contact with students which is of a sexually motivated or physically abusive nature, or any type of inappropriate touching or physical assault.

- Teachers/staff may never forbid students from sharing any conversations or information with parents or administration, nor instruct students to "keep secrets" from their parents.

- Teachers/staff may not invite any student, explicitly or indirectly, to engage in inappropriate activities, especially if such invitation is accompanied by a promise to reward the student for complying or a threat to punish the student for not complying.

- Teachers/staff must refrain from any immodest behavior or speech, especially from exhibiting sexual interest in students and any other form of inappropriate speech.

Failure to comply with any of these standards constitutes a violation of school policy and should be immediately reported to the principal, who should take appropriate action. Such action may include, under appropriate circumstances, reporting to the civil authorities when the principal determines that there is reason to believe that inappropriate activity has in fact occurred, insofar as halacha and secular law require such reporting.

Every school, in consultation with a competent Moreh hora'ah, attorney and mental health professional, is required to develop internal procedures for dealing with these issues.

Guidelines of Orthodox Organizations

Torah u'Mesora: Declaration of Rabbinical Board

Elul 5763

At recent meetings of the Rabbinical Board of Torah U'Mesorah, attended by Rav Dovid Feinstein, Rav Yitzchok Feigelstock, Rav Aharon Feldman, Rav Shmuel Kamenetsky, Rav Aryeh Malkiel Kotler, Rav Avrohom Chaim Levin, Rav Yaakov Perlow and Rav Aaron Schechter, shlita, the following statement concerning a painful issue was issued:

We address ourselves to the problem of child molestation in our community. A small number of individuals have caused untold pain to many children, primarily varying in age from three to fourteen. In addition to the sins which they have committed, they have created painful memories in the minds of their victims, memories which can have a devastating lifetime impact.

It is incumbent upon everyone to use every means to stop these violations of children, including, at times, exposing the identities of the abusers and even their incarceration. At times, our primary intent may not be to punish the perpetrators, but rather to help them. Therefore it is preferable, wherever appropriate, to force them to undergo appropriate professional therapy.

Torah U'Mesorah is issuing a set of behavioral and reporting standards for principals to implement in their yeshivos and day schools, which, it is hoped, will strengthen the protection of students. It is well documented that molesters are rarely strangers to the child; they are usually relatives or neighbors – and in rare occasions, even teachers. They are able to act because they have the child's confidence, and then, after the act, they usually threaten him or her with punishment if he or she reveals what has occurred or they shame their victims into keeping a secret.

It is important that parents advise children in an appropriate manner to beware of potential molesters. Children must be told to advise their parents of any abusive behavior, and assured that they will suffer no consequences if they do so. We encourage rabbanim throughout our communities to address this issue, which, in itself, will serve as a deterrent to potential abusers. Rabbanim must also help and support anyone who has fallen victim to abuse, as well as refer them to seek professional help from frum private practitioners and/or organizations in their

Child & Domestic Abuse

community. It goes without saying that rabbanim should take precautions that accusations are not made maliciously or without basis.

*Practical guide of what to do

1. Protecting victim is more important than protecting reputations

Contrary to common belief, the primary concern of halacha is the well being of the victim – not protecting the reputation of others. Rav Sternbuch said that present or future victims must be protected even if it hurts the reputation of a community, family or individuals. He also said that the centrality of this concern for the victim also means that even if institutions such as yeshivos will suffer financial damage because of the disclosure - the victim's welfare still takes precedence. Of course if it is possible to protect the victim without causing any harm to others – then it is obligatory to use the more benign approach. The halachic imperative to save the victim simply means that the well-being of the victim is not sacrificed to protect the reputation or financial well being of others.

2. Obligation to victim doesn't end with reporting the crime

The reporting of abuse to family, rabbi or even the police does not remove the halachic obligation to make sure that the victim is protected. In other words if the reporting of the abuse to others does not actually result in the protection of the victim, the obligation still remains on those who know about the abuse to do something. They are required to try to create a mechanism for protection – whether it means contacting or hiring experts or forming new community organizations. Reporting the abuse to others is only a possible means to protection and thus only has significance if it in fact protects the present and future victims from the molester.

3. Reporting the molester, mandated reporting & jail sentences

Since it is almost always the case that family, school, or community are incapable of preventing the perpetrator from continuing his abuse, therefore the police or social services must be informed to protect children from the molester. In addition, if the secular law mandates the reporting of abuse or even suspicions of abuse – then the Torah requires that we comply with that law. The possibility or even the certainty that the perpetrator will be sent to jail is an insufficient concern to refrain from reporting a molester. That is because the poskim say that today a jail sentence is not life

Child & Domestic Abuse

threatening. Some poskim are even more stringent and say that he should be sent to jail - even if it is possibly life threatening - in order to protect the victim

4. Discard advice of rabbi/social services – if it doesn't protect victim

The protection of the victim is the halachic imperative. Therefore Rav Sternbuch told me that if a person receives a psak from a rabbi which clearly doesn't protect the victim – that rabbi's psak should be ignored. Rav Sternbuch told me that such a rabbi is not acting as a rabbi and that one should find another rabbi whose advice will protect. Thus one is not allowed to accept a psak from a talmid chachom - and is required to ask another rabbi - if the psak will not protect the children. There is no requirement to show respect to the first rabbi's psak if it means sacrificing your child. It is a well-established principle, that if a rabbi errs in a dvar mishna (a clear cut halacha) that one does not have to listen to him. Therefore if a child is being molested, and a rabbi says not to call the police – you should find another rabbi who will say to go to the police or social services. Furthermore if reporting is mandated by secular law, the police or social services should be informed. Similarly if a therapist or even the police do not provide a means of protecting the victim, then it is your responsibility to find other people or ways that protect the children. Your responsibility is not simply to report the matter – but to actually bring about protection for the victims.

5. Rabbis are only to be consulted first - if no immediate danger

If abuse is not likely to happen immediately and there is time to consult with a rabbi, or principal – then it is best to do so. It is important to respect the authorities in society. However not only must they be knowledgeable about abuse but they also need to consult with mental health professionals who are experts in abuse to determine how to deal with the situation. However showing respect to religious and community authorities is only required when it can be done without endangering the child. If there is possible immediate danger and the delay in contacting the police might be harmful - then the police should be contacted immediately even if the rabbi has not been consulted.

6. Rabbis & Torah community need police & social services

The problem of abuse can not be handled exclusively by community leaders or rabbis – despite assertions that are sometimes made that they are the only ones

Practical guide of what to do

authorized by Jewish law and that the police and social services are to be avoided. Claims that secular authorities must be excluded because of chilul hashem, lashon harah, mesira and the prohibition of using non-Jewish courts – are simply not valid as demonstrated by the extensive citations quoted in this sefer. Rather the prime concern in abuse is how to protect the individual and community from harm. At the same time, it is important to involve and utilize rabbinic and community leaders since they have unique and valuable resources and authority. There is no reason – in Jewish or secular law - that the religious and secular authorities can't form a partnership. This has been in fact done by Rav Yehuda Silman – member of Rav Nisson Karelitz's beis din – in Bnei Brak.

7. Protecting victim from harm is primary – not punishing the abuser

In contemporary society, dealing with a molester is primarily an issue of how to protect the victim. It is not a judiciary issue in which rabbis must judge the guilt or innocence of the accused and decide on punishment. This is a point that Rav Yehuda Silman has repeatedly made. In a non-judicial framework there is no halachic requirement of first seeking the guidance of a rabbi, beis din or even proper witnesses. Knowledge of the facts does not have to be absolute in order to act. This knowledge can come from rumors, the testimony of women and children as well as non-Jews. Rav Sternbuch told me that the reason for consulting a rabbi is basically, "so that the world is not hefker (lawless)." However, this consideration is not more important than obtaining protection. When seeking protection, there is no need to utilize only observant religious Jews. This is clearly stated in the classic Torah literature. If a rabbi claims that nothing can be done to protect the victim because of the prohibition against informing (mesira) or chilul hashem or lashon harah – Rav Sternbuch told me that his view should be ignored. Such a psak for inaction and passivity is unequivocally wrong because it is contrary to the mainstream Torah authorities throughout history - as is obvious from the sources cited in this sefer.

8. Investigation required for all claims - even rumors

Rav Sternbuch said that the halacha requires that all claims and even rumors of abuse must be investigated. It is necessary to ascertain who the abuser is and the exact nature of the abuse. Abuse often produces severe long-term psychological damage and trauma and increases the likelihood of suicide. However much of this damage is often not apparent in the early stages of the abuse – and therefore requires expert evaluation.

Child & Domestic Abuse

The damage and trauma of abuse not only severely affects the victim's future marriage and children, but all of his/her personal, social and professional interactions thoughts his/her lifetime as well.

Not only is it necessary to determine whether abuse is happening but it is necessary to ascertain the severity, frequency and likelihood of future abuse. Furthermore it is important to ascertain whether the abuse is life threatening, or likely to cause severe psychological or physical damage. Abuse between two 6 years olds playing doctor is not to be treated as abuse being done by a violent adult sex predator or that done by a pedophile who is also a pediatrician.

The preliminary investigation is typically done by family or teachers, however in fact it is preferable that it should be done by a mental health professional who is an expert in abuse. Not only can the damage of abuse to the victim be strongly compounded by incompetent investigation but memories can be distorted or even created by asking inappropriate, leading or judgmental questions. The investigator needs as a minimum to know how to ask the questions and what to look for – while providing support for the victim. While a rabbi should be consulted, he should be someone who is experienced and knowledgeable in this area. Even so, it is still best if he works together with an experienced mental health worker or organization. The validity of halachic judgments is dependent upon knowledge of the psychological reality.

The investigation needs to be conducted with great sensitivity and total respect for the privacy and reputation of all concerned. It is halachically prohibited to use accusations of abuse as an excuse for character assassination or even casual gossip. As Rav Moshe Halberstam (Yeshurun 15 page 651) points out, even if a person is in fact guilty of abuse – his family has not committed any crime. Therefore utmost care need to be taken to minimize harming and degrading his family

9. Rabbi needs be supportive & display empathy to the victim

It is crucial that the rabbi consulted be supportive of the victim (and his family) in both attitude and constructive actions. Furthermore a rabbi, as an authority figure, can cause much damage by conveying suspicions that the victim is responsible or that there is something evil or sinful in reporting the abuse in the first place. It is also harmful if he indicates that he thinks the victim is lying. Therefore the rabbi's reaction

Practical guide of what to do

– whether positive and supportive or negative and rejecting - can make or break the victim. This greatly impacts on the effectiveness of the required rehabilitation process

10. Social pressure and/or rabbinic pressure against reporting

It is very devastating that despite having your child molested, and despite being told by your rabbi to call the police – there will usually be tremendous social pressure not to report the abuse. Sometimes there is more than social pressure. There might be violence and the children are sometimes forced out of school and the family driven out of the community. There will be opponents - including rabbis - who will indignantly claim that according to the Torah reporting abuse is one of the worst sins. And this despite the clear and consistent proof to the contrary - by the overwhelming consensus of halachic authorities - reported in this sefer. Many people buckle under this pressure and end up gratuitously sacrificing their children However the Mishna Berura (Biur Halacha 1:1) and others exhort that one must be brazen as a leopard to fight against social pressure from those who don't want you to do the right thing (Avos 5:3).

11. Victim must actually be protected – not just given promises

The halacha requires that a reliable way to protect society must be found. While it might be possible for a school principal or rabbi to place restrictions on a teacher who is abusing students – there is no way of guaranteeing that he won't in fact continue abusing students in the school or outside the school or that he won't simply move to a new community and continue preying on children. Abusers are known to be skilled liars and are very skilled at circumventing restrictions that prevent them from fulfilling their lusts. Sometimes the abuse takes place because an opportunity presents itself. However studies about abusers reveal that in most instances the molester does not simply lose control on one occasion. Rather his deviance is a compulsion and addiction that motivates him to abuse even hundreds of victims. Victims are not necessarily chosen at random but might be cultivated by the molesters for an extended period of time before he attacks them. Not only are there many victims but each victim might be abused repeatedly. This is a pattern that typically repeats itself in the different communities that the abuser lives in over his lifetime. Thus finding a reliable way of protection against the molester is very problematic and is best left to those who are experienced experts.

Child & Domestic Abuse

12. Call police immediately for danger or suspected danger

If the abuse appears to be life threatening or to cause severe psychological or physical damage then the police or social service department must be called immediately – even if this leads to arrest and lengthy imprisonment of the molester. Even if the victims seem to be fine – a professional mental health worker needs to provide an evaluation since the result of trauma is often repressed and doesn't manifest itself for years.

13. Molesters are typically friends or family of victim

Pedophiles and molesters are individuals who are indistinguishable from the general population on psychological measures. In general they don't look evil or apparently act evil. However they have a lust for children which usually doesn't disappear and often reoccurs even 10 years or more after being dormant – even following imprisonment and punishment for these crimes. It is important to remember that most abuse is done by someone the child knows – not a malevolent stranger. The abuser is also typically not the stereotypic weird or mentally ill fiend. They might in fact be loving parents (and spouses) and distinguished teachers and leaders to most other children – just not to those that they select as their victims. Unfortunately many molesters also view themselves as caring and loving individuals even when they are abusing their victims. Indeed, this is indicative of their distorted thinking. In reality, they are concerned only with their own lusts when they deceptively act as a mentor or friend to the lonely or shy child that they abuse.

14. Incest victims need to be evaluated for foster care

If the abuse involves incest with a parent then the child needs to be separated from the parent – even if it means foster care. If it involves relatives such as an uncle or sibling – then evaluation of the family needs to be done to ascertain whether the family is a healthy environment for the child. It is not unusual in the case of incest with a father, that the mother knows about it but is too weak and overwhelmed to protect her child.

15. Child's or subordinate's consent is not considered consent

If the abuse is being done by an authority figure, such as a rabbi or teacher – even if there is "consent" – this is not considered as consent. The adult is considered responsible despite the fact that it is not uncommon for the adult to complain that he

Practical guide of what to do

was seduced. In general, when there is clear difference in status, such as an employer, army officer, psychologist, rabbi or teacher – the one with the inferior status is assumed to have less control and freedom in the relationship and is more likely to be harmed and traumatized even if they gave their "consent". Thus the one with superior status is to be assumed responsible for the improper relationship.

16. Adult-youth sexual relations must be stopped & reported

Even if sexual relations are happening between an adult and a male older than 13 or a girl older than 12 – it can not be considered free will and of full consent - and it needs to be stopped. Similar sexual relations between teenagers above the age of 12/13 needs to be stopped or between teenagers and children need to be stopped. It makes no difference whether an adult woman is having sexual relations with a male child or youth or a man is having sexual relations with a female child or youth. Whether this needs to be reported to the police depends on whether it represents an ongoing threat to the well being of the children or youths as determined by the evaluation of an expert mental health professional. If should also be reported if the secular law considers it a crime and mandates reporting it.

17. Uncertain abuser (sofek rodef) is also reported

Rav Silman has poskened that there is no distinction between reporting an abuser or an uncertain abuser. A sofek rodef is treated as a certain rodef. Similarly if there is a question whether someone did teshuva or whether after a number of years he seems to have controlled his lusts – it is better to make the choice which protects the child - and the molester is not trusted again with children. It is important to understand that the sickness of pedophilia is a life long condition and therefore even with old age his desires are not necessarily diminished. Even those who have been imprisoned and received psychotherapy, have been found to sometimes renew abusing even 20 or thirty years later! Therefore it can not be presumed that an abuser has learned his lesson and is now controlling his lusts. He is to be considered a danger to children unless a careful psychological/physiological evaluation verifies that his lust has disappeared.

18. Crime should ideally be reported by the victim or his family

Halachically it is best if the victim or the victim's immediate family were the ones to report the abuse when required. However if they are not able to or unwilling to –

Child & Domestic Abuse

then it must be done by everyone else. The Maharach Ohr Zarua (142) explains that this is a way of dealing with the greater anger that the personally involved parties have. The Taz (C.M. 421:13) explains that if a concerned citizen, upon attempting to rescue someone, causes more damage than was minimally necessary to save someone he is liable. However a potential victim or his/her family are not required to give a measured response to a rodef and are not liable for an excessive response. This is simply recognition that concerning self-defense or defending a family member it is much harder to be objective and therefore more leeway is given. The Taz bases this on the Rosh and Tur. This is not to be construed as meaning that the family has a greater obligation to help and therefore non-relatives can avoid the responsibility. Everyone in fact has an equal obligation to protect and rescue others.

19. All abuse – even not explicitly in the Torah – must be stopped

Even if there is no sexual intercourse but there is viewing of pornography, sexual caressing, exposure of genitals, or other activities that the abuser does to obtain sexual satisfaction from the victim – this has to be stopped immediately and measures instituted to prevent it from reoccurring. If there is mandated reporting on these matters then it must be reported. If it involves a teacher, the teacher must be prevented from teaching. All such perpetrators must be prevented henceforth from having unsupervised association with children. These types of experiences can cause lifelong psychological damage and trauma, not only for children but for teenagers and adults, as well – even if they claim they participated willingly.

20. Strong rumors alone necessitates removing teacher

Even if there are only persistent rumors that a teacher is an abuser – he must be removed from his job – unless it can be shown that he is being victimized by enemies or a malicious student.

21. False accusations are rarely made by children

Even though false reports and accusations do occur – the overwhelming majority of cases of a child accusing an adult of abuse are valid. The reason being that the child, in order to express him/herself, must muster considerable fortitude and courage in the face of the tremendous embarrassment and severe repercussions that typically results from such accusations. While this is apparently changing in the secular world,

Practical guide of what to do

it is still true in the religious world - especially for girls. But even in the secular world studies indicate that children rarely make up false accusations that they were abused

False accusation when they do occur, must often happen when an untrained adult deduces that there was abuse and influences the child and others through improper investigation and questioning. This is why investigation needs to be handled by trained professionals.

22. Schools need to develop programs

If the abuse is between children who can be readily controlled by parents and/or teachers and these adults will definitely take responsibility - then there is no need to immediately call the police. A mental health professional should be consulted. It is important that the school and community provide a program to educate the children that abuse (whether sexual or bullying) is wrong and to monitor their behavior to see that they obey. The program needs to be developed under the guidance and with the approval of rabbinic and mental health experts as well as teachers and parents.

23. Molesters need to be publicized to protect children

It is necessary to publicize the names or at least the existence of molesters in order that people can protect their children. This should be carried out in an organized manner by people who have been designated by the community in coordination with rabbinical supervisors and mental health professionals. A small investment in prevention is preferable to treatment after the tragedy of abuse.

There is a need to communicate information about abusers and suspected abusers to responsible individuals in other communities. It is wrong to think that forcing an abuser out of your community or school is enough. The community to where the abuser moves has to also know about him to protect itself. This needs to be supervised by rabbinic experts and mental health professionals. Instead of simply forcing the molester to move elsewhere where he is not known – it is best if he is dealt with in a community that knows him. Not only must the molester be dealt with, but there needs to be a mechanism for reporting and punishing those who enable the molester to continue to abuse and/or to escape punishment and treatment. This includes those who intimidate witnesses or victims or conceal evidence.

Child & Domestic Abuse

24. Molester's access to children must be restricted

It is necessary to restrict access of molesters to children – even if they have served prison sentences and surely if they have not. This means that they are unemployable in schools or public places such as pizza parlors. They are not to be involved in child care nor are they to provide private lessons or counseling. If they can't be stopped from this employment for legal reasons - then they need to be governed by very strict regulations and they need to be carefully supervised at all times. Any supervision must include some means of actual verification that it is effective.

25. Clear protocol of response must be developed with police

Ideally the community leaders and rabbis need to have an on going (formal and close) relationship with the police and social services. This also means that each community should have designated individuals –therapists or rabbis - who can provide access to the resources of both the community and the secular government to deal properly with these problems. Dealing with abusers is difficult – both for the community alone or for the secular agencies alone. Both have abilities and knowledge that are best utilized by working together. So even if an abuser has been arrested, he might not be sent to jail and the secular system might not carefully monitor his activities. The community however does have the organizational ability and knowledge to provide this critical oversight. On the other hand the community does not have the power that the secular agencies have to control the abuser. Ideally a person who suspects abuse should need to know a single telephone number or individual who will interface with this cooperative endeavor. Too much harm and inactivity results from not knowing what to do or being accused of speaking lashon harah or violating the prohibition of being an informant – by those who have an incorrect knowledge of these halachos.

*Synopsis of HaRav Moshe Sternbuch's views

This synopsis was written after I discussed these issues with HaRav Sternbuch. He reviewed it and wrote comments - which are included here in bold type. He approved it for publication.

We need to acknowledge that our communities have a serious abuse problem. While our problem is not more serious than that of non-Jews - it is still not acceptable. The abuse includes not only spousal abuse, but also physical and sexual abuse of children. Unfortunately there have been many mistakes made in dealing with this problem in the past - including those made by well meaning teachers, principals, and community leaders. This was due primarily to the concern that publicizing these incidents would harm the reputation of the community and community institutions - as well as the other members of the family. There was also a mistaken belief that there was little permanent harm done to the victims by the abuse. It was believed that those who were beaten, molested or raped would get over the abuse with time. In general it was believed that the collateral damage to the reputations of others was more harmful and embarrassing than the damage and shame to the victim. It was not unusual for the community to force the abuser to move to another neighborhood and tell the victim and their family not to reveal these incidents - especially to the social agencies or police. It was not unusual for a teacher to be fired - and not tell the new school that hired him about his problem. It was not unheard of for a family of a victim that reported the molester to be ostracized and driven from the community because of their disregard for the welfare of the community. Thus the prime strategy for dealing with the problem of abuse in the past was to sweep it under the rug.

However it has become evident in the last few years that this approach is mistaken. The victims of abuse - whether it is a battered wife or a molested child - suffer horribly. The psychological damage doesn't get forgotten and in fact often causes harm for the rest of the victim's life. Equally as bad is that typically the molesters went on to abuse others - despite promises to stop and to repent.

Child & Domestic Abuse

It is time to acknowledge the mistakes of the past and to correct them. To accomplish this we need to focus on three essential Torah values. The Torah emphasizes our obligation 1) to love everyone (Vayikra 19: 18), 2) to protect him or her Vayikra (19: 16) from harm and 3) to restore those who have been harmed to normal existence (Devarim 22:2). Shabbos (31a) states clearly that that which is hateful to you don't do it to others and that this is the entire Torah - the rest being just commentary. Mishlei (3: 17) says that the ways of the Torah are pleasantness.

In order to deal correctly with these serious dangers, we need to remember a number of elementary Torah basics. 1) The Torah is concerned that families and communities are places of nurturing love and security. 2) The halacha is clear that an innocent person is not sacrificed to save others - whether concerning life or physical or sexual abuse. A child or wife is not to be silenced in order that the reputation of the family, yeshiva or community might be preserved. In fact Rav Moshe Sternbuch told me that a rabbi that asserts such a thing is not speaking as a rabbi and his views should be ignored. If a rabbi states such an opinion, Rav Sternbuch told me that another rabbi - who understands the centrality of the helping the victim – should be consulted. 3) Furthermore the inevitable exposure of the systematic covering up the truth and ignoring the anguish of the victims is a much greater chilul HaShem then the fact that the Jews suffers from abuse like the rest of the world. In our modern age - the misguided practice of cover-ups - also doesn't even work because of easy of communication with the telephone, news media and Internet.

The principles we discuss apply to all abuse - whether spousal or child. We will be discussing how the Torah, psychology and secular law relate to the abuse and abuser as well as the range of legitimate halachic responses. We address the questions of how to protect potential and actual victims and how to investigate the identity of the perpetrator. We discuss the obligation to provide treatment to both the victim and perpetrator and the issue of punishment of the perpetrator.

We are also concerned with the serious problem of how to protect people as well as punishing the perpetrators - when the traditional beis din and community has little power. Despite this lack of power there is an absolute obligation to be subordinate to rabbinical authority. At the same time the power and the ability to do something useful is in reality in the secular social agencies and law system. However the legitimacy of the secular system for an Orthodox Jew is dependent on rabbinic

Synopsis – with comments by HaRav Sternbuch

authorization. In sum, that which has legitimacy has no independent power and that which has power has no independent legitimacy.

This is not an exhaustive or final word on the subject, but a serious attempt to give a broad understanding of the topic. The need for this information is not only for the therapists who deal directly with the victims of abuse the perpetrators but also for parents, teachers and rabbis who are not yet aware of how serious the problem is nor the variety of legitimate halachic responses. In sum, the goal of this work is to inform and sensitize everyone to the problem of abuse as well as the halachic concerns and remedies.

Let me list some general basic issues of dealing with abuse. Ideally each case should be dealt with experts - both from the rabbinic and psychological aspects including the relevant government social agencies - and the police contacted when needed. In addition the community should have a program not only of responding to abuse but also to prevent it.

Need to investigate all rumors and charges of abuse

Any and all rumors about abuse should be investigated. The laws of lashon harah do not prohibit investigation and informing relevant people of potential harm. Rav Sternbuch (Teshuvos v'Hanhagos 5:398) presents a detailed discussion of this matter.

Pischei Tshuva (O.C. 156) states: I want to note here that while all the books of mussar are greatly concerned about the sin of lashon harah, I am greatly concerned about the opposite problem. I want to protest about the even greater and more common sin of refraining from speaking negatively when it is necessary to save someone from being harmed. For example if you saw a person waiting in ambush to kill someone or breaking into someone's house or store at night. Is it conceivable that you would refrain from notifying the intended victim to protect himself from the assailant - because of the prohibition of speaking lashon harah? By not saying anything you commit the unbearable sin of transgressing the prohibition of Vayikra (19: 16): Do not speak lashon harah [but] do not stand idly by when the blood of your fellow man is threatened? By not speaking up, you violate the mitzva of returning that which is lost to its owner Devarim (22:2).

Child & Domestic Abuse

The first thing a real posek asks is, "What are the facts."

Rav Moshe Sternbuch told me in the name of Rav Yechezkeil Abramsky that a posek first has to establish the facts. He needs to use his seichal and commonsense before he starts applying halachic factors. He said, for example, that when a rav is dealing with a case of agunah he first needs to ask whether it seems that the husband is alive or dead. After he clarifies the facts, he then asks what is the halacha in this case and what should be done.

Similarly in cases of abuse, first it is needed to establish what is actually happening. We need to establish whether abuse is occurring. Is the child in pain? Is the abuse likely to reoccur or was it a onetime occurrence. Is he or his parents misinterpreting innocent events? Is she angry or being coached by an angry parent in the middle of a hostile divorce? If he is being abused, what is the nature of the abuse and who is doing the abuse? After the reality has been determined, the halachic questions can be asked.

Protection of society sometimes requires emergency laws

The Shulchan Aruch (C.M. 1) states that because of absence of not having true rabbinic ordination and the loss of the Temple, there are many crimes which we cannot judge according to Torah law. However Shulchan Aruch (C.M. 2) says that there is an additional fundamental principle. That is a community has the right to survive and its citizens have the right to peace and tranquility. Therefore because of this emergency need, the community has a right to do whatever it needs in terms of punishing criminals and accepting evidence that it deems is needed for its well being. Rashba (3:393): "My view is that if the witnesses are believed by the judges, then it is permitted to punish the accused financially or physically depending upon what the judges think is appropriate to be beneficial to society. Because if we insist on doing only what is specified by Torah law and not to punish except as specified in the Torah - the world will end up destroyed. That is because the elementary rules of a functioning society will be breached and consequently it will be ruined. It is an established practice to punish those who physically harm others ... Every community makes judgments in order to preserve it and this is true in every generation and every place according to what is perceived as the needs of the times." This also expressed in Bava Metzia (83a).

Synopsis – with comments by HaRav Sternbuch

Circumstantial evidence & testimony of women & children

The poskim permit the use of circumstantial evidence in these cases as we see in Bava Metzia (83a) where R' Eliezer the son of R' Shimon bar Yochai caught thieves for the Roman government in order to protect society. This is stated in the Rashba and Shulchan Aruch (C.M. 2), Shulchan Aruch (C.M. 35:14) and Ritva (Bava Metzia 84a) as well as contemporary authorities such as Rav Yehuda Silman and Rav Eliashiv.

Mesira (informing) the secular authorities

The greatest reason for people refusing to get involved in these cases is that they are afraid of the serious crime of informing (moser). It is one of the worst crimes a Jew can do. A moser is someone who causes a Jew or his property to be given to non-Jews or the secular government. Shulchan Aruch (C.M. 388:9) says an informer has no portion in the World to Come and he is not considered a Jew (Shulchan Aruch (Y.D. 281: 3). However there is no question that mesira does not apply in the case of rodef when someone's life is in danger or the perpetrator is committing a sin that is punished by kares or capital punishment. There are many poskim who permit turning for protection to the police or government agencies. These include Rambam (Hilchos Chovel u'Mazik 8: 11) the Rema (388:7), the Shach (388:45), the Sema (388:30) and many others. The Chasam Sofer (Gittin 7a) also permits informing the police or social agencies even when the abuse is only monetary or not life-threatening. This is also agreed upon by Minchas Yitzchok (8:148). [There is also the Tzitz Eliezer (19:52) which is based on the Aruch HaShulchan (388:7) which says that there is no prohibition to day since we have an equitable government. However there is evidence (Aruch HaShulchan 342: 1) that he said this only because of the fear of the censor]. In sum the majority of poskim permit going to the police when there is a clear threat of physical or sexual abuse. **Rav Sternbuch noted, "However a Rabbinical authority should be consulted as we discuss later."**

Mandatory governmental reporting

Shmuel (Nedarim 28a) said that the law of the land is the law. Most poskim hold that this principle is a Torah obligation. In many countries the law is clear that any suspected child abuse is required to be reported - at least by doctors, teachers and psychologist. Thus it would follow that complying with government mandated reported is a Torah obligation – assuming it doesn't involve transgressing clear halachic prohibitions. Furthermore failure to comply with mandated reporting laws

Child & Domestic Abuse

can result in monetary fines as well as jail sentences. In addition a person is vulnerable to law suits for damage resulting from failure to report.

The obligation to comply with government mandated reporting is learned from Bava Metzia (83a) where R' Eliezer informed on Jewish thieves to the Roman government based on circumstantial evidence – to save innocent people from being harmed. Those arrested were executed. In a similar case the gemora reports that R' Yishmael justified his actions by saying it was required by the king. Thus it is clear that when the government requires reporting of child molesting or even suspected molestation that there is a requirement to comply – just because the government requires it.

In addition a dangerous person – such as a wild driver – is also required to be reported to the police by the poskim because of the law of rodef. A child molester is also a dangerous person.

Obviously if there is a possibility of consulting with a rav before reporting - without anyone suffering harm - it is necessary to do so. This is especially true when the sanctions against failure to report are not strictly enforced or they do not involve a significant amount of money. In addition, when a significant penalty - either of money or jail - is imposed as punishment for failure to report - a posek needs to be consulted where the reporting involves transgressing halacha.

But where there is a reasonable possibility of harm resulting when consulting a rav first – then it is clear that reporting should be done first. The prime consideration is preventing harm to the child or abused wife.

Aiva - causing hatred to Jews - is reason to report abuse

If the non-reporting of abuse causes hatred toward Jews, then that is another reason why it is required to report.

Consulting rabbi before calling social services or police

Despite the fact that the halacha is clear that a child molester should be reported to the police and in fact it is often required by secular law - the poskim generally state that a rabbi should be consulted first. It is obvious of course that if waiting to consult a rabbi results in danger or harm to the child - that the police should be informed without consulting a rabbi. In the normal case where there is time, however, why

Synopsis – with comments by HaRav Sternbuch

should it be necessary to consult a rabbi? Rav Sternbuch commented that where there are serious consequences of making a mistake - it is required that a rabbi be consulted for the sake of objectivity. Even if there is little chance of making a mistake, he said that a rabbi needs to be consulted "so the world should not be hefker (without structure and authority)."

In addition in this area besides the danger of misunderstanding information, there is also the possibility of false accusations. Students who want to settle a score with teachers or divorcing couples whose lawyers advise them to make false accusations to gain custody are a danger which a rabbi can help prevent. In most cases there is no danger to a child by consulting a rav first and if there is concern that there will be then the police should be contacted. It is always best to consult a rabbi who has a lot of experience in these matters and especially once who has close relations with mental health professions and government social agencies and the police. Even after consulting a psychologist or lawyer, a rabbi should still be consulted before going to the police. Not just because of the reasons already discussed, but also as protection against those who mistakenly consider all informing the police as being prohibited. These elements can not only harass those who go to the police but they can cause severe damage to them by their slander and criticism of the entire family.

Rejecting a rabbi's psak when he says not to go to the police

One frequently encountered problem is when there is clear evidence of child abuse and yet the rabbi consulted says not to go to the police. He might say that the molester promised never to do it again or that the molester's family or community or yeshiva might suffer significant financial losses or embarrassment. In other words if the rabbi is saying to sacrifice children for the sake of money or embarrassment or the disgrace to the community, it is clear however that this view has no basis in Jewish law. We don't sacrifice innocent people for the sake of negative consequences to others. **Rav Moshe Sternbuch commented that any rav who would say such a thing is not practicing as a rav. A rabbi has an obligation to provide protection to the victim. By definition it seems it is an unjust ruling. Any rabbi who makes such a ruling may be ignorant of either the halacha or he doesn't understand what the molesting or wife abuse causes. Therefore if there is time - another rabbi should be consulted.**

Child & Domestic Abuse

However an alternative reason that a rabbi might say not to report the molester is that he feels he can guarantee protection for children against the molester. For example he might threaten the molester with a severe beating or provides supervision or he claims the molester has repented and won't abuse again. He might also claim he can provide therapy equal or better to a psychologist. While these seem to be logically equivalent to the police, the likelihood that they will be effective is not very high. Therefore one should find a competent rabbi who agrees that the police should be informed in the case of actual abuse. **Rav Sternbuch commented that only a known talmid chachom posek can posken these problems.**

Chemical castration - treatment not punishment

The law of rodef is that he is to be stopped from his crime with the minimal intervention. Thus if physical force is needed - one can not use more than is needed and if he is killed when he could have been stopped by lesser means - the one who killed him is viewed as having done the sinner of murder. **Rav Sternbuch commented that if the only way to stop him from rape is castration maybe he could be castrated. It is preferred to use chemical castration rather then surgical castration. However this is a serious problem and a rav must be consulted.**

Social sanctions - burial, aliya or minyan

What sanctions can be applied to a molester who has not been arrested and refuses to be in treatment and are unrepentant?. Such people should be subjected to social sanctions that are referred to as nidoi or cherem and are described in Shulchan Aruch (Y.D. 334). The rabbi of the community could publicize that he is a molester so that children can be kept away from him. Sanctions include not counting him as part of minyan or honoring by calling him up to the Torah or allowing him to lead prayers. He should not be allowed to be a witness or serve as a judge. **Rav Sternbuch commented that he is not eulogized.**

Teshuva (repentance) - encourage by not reporting molesting?

Our Sages felt it important to encourage repentance. For example there was a rabbinic decree made that if someone stole a wooden beam and built a house with it - that it was not necessary to rip down the house to return it to its original owner. Despite the Torah obligation to restore the original object, the Rabbis said it was just necessary to compensate the victim

Synopsis – with comments by HaRav Sternbuch

with the value. A second rabbinic decree was that if a person offered to make restitution on something he stole, the money was not to be accepted.

Finally the Sages said that it is a Torah prohibition to remind someone of their sinful past. This is also to encourage repentance since the person realizes his past deeds will be forgotten.

Given this concern for encouraging repentance, what should be the status of an abuser who claims to have repented? Should a child molester who has not abused anyone in 15 years be reported to the police? Should he be recorded in a database of sex offenders? Clearly there are abusers who are unlikely to sin again - should they be treated in the same way as someone who is still an active molester? **Rav Sternbuch commented that it seems that Jewish Law would not allow such a case to be reported.**

The greatest question, however is whether someone who has raped children be reported to the police - despite the fact that he claims he won't molest another child and is willing to go for therapy, chemical castration and community supervision? It is obvious that according to secular law he must be reported. **Rav Sternbuch commented that Jewish Law could be decided only after consultation with a competent Rabbinical Authority.**

Abortion in the case of rape and incest

Pregnancy in the case of rape or incest is a very serious and complex issue. It not only is dangerous because of the constant reminder of degradation and pain but also carrying for a child from rape and incest has many negative issues including increased suicide and danger of harm to the child. Therefore a gadol needs to be consulted as to, what to do. **Rav Sternbuch commented that in general, abortion is a very serious crime in Jewish Law and is rarely permitted.**

Background checking - Database and fingerprinting

Should there be a database of all criminals that is available to the general public? Even if there is a general public database, should yeshivos utilize it to check all employees? Furthermore should the database include fingerprints so that all employees are fingerprinted to prevent getting a job under a false name? Or should it be enough for a person to provide evidence of qualification for a job and personal references? It would seem that such a data base is desirable - even if it would add to the expenses of the institution and would prevent a person from covering up their past. In the public schools in New York, children are protected by mandatory fingerprinting and backgrounds checks on all employees. No one can be

Child & Domestic Abuse

employed if they have a history of sexual abuse and anyone discovered to be an abuser after being: hired is automatically fired. There is mandatory reporting of incidents to the social welfare agencies and police. There are also data basis of sexual abusers that are checked. **Rav Sternbuch commented that rabbis should decide what is needed for each yeshiva.**

Jewish calculus – to stop sin or suffering?

I have spent much time researching and analyzing the issue of abuse and reaction to suffering. The issue that keeps reoccurring is why is so little being done to alleviate or even give comfort to abuse victims. Originally I assumed that the issue was a simple halachic issue - the problem of mesira or chillul hashem or the complicated halachos of lashon harah.

While these reasons obviously play a part I have come to the conclusion that what is at work in our community is a theological attitude or value. This issue is stated clearly in Sanhedrin (73a) concerning the issue of stopping a rodef (someone pursuing someone to kill or rape). The Mishna says, "these are those who are saved by their lives". This is an ambiguous statement. Who is saved? There are commentaries that say the reference is to the pursuer - we kill this pursuer to save his soul from sin. Others say that it means we save the potential victim by killing the pursuer.

It seems that we have two alternative lenses for evaluating these events. Are we preventing someone from sinning or are we saving a person from attack. As I have used these two lenses over a wide variety of issues - it seems in fact that this is the answer to my original question. Are we concerning with stopping sin and thus we are concerned with maximizing the spiritual content of our universe? Or alternatively am I concerned with the human suffering of the victim.

A clear example of the orthogonality of these views is the well known story of Rabbi Akiva. He died a horrible death of his skin being shredded with iron combs. Rabbi Akiva was ecstatic that he could die such a horrible painful death because of its spiritual significance. In contrast his students and even the angels didn't understand this. They were bothered by the human element that he was suffering a horrible death.

Another example is Sma (C.M. 421:13) who mentions that a person is allowed to save another person from being beaten - even if it entails beating the assailant. He says that is because we need to stop the assailant from sinning. However he says if a person normally ignores such events and in general doesn't stop assailants from

Child & Domestic Abuse

beating other people it shows he is not concerned about stopping sinning. Therefore he says he can not intervene or rather if he intervenes he needs to pay because his motivation was not to stop sin but rather he hated the assailant. (The Taz comments on the Sema and says he doesn't understand what relevancy the intent is. As long as the victim is saved from beating - that is sufficient to allow the rescuer to beat the assailant.)

Correspondingly the Chofetz Chaim says that even though lashon harah can be said if it brings benefit - but even if there is a beneficial outcome to speaking lashon harah - it is prohibited to say lashon harah. The Klausenberger explains that the evilness of lashon harah is dependent on the intent of the speaker - not the consequences. This would mean that if a woman is raped and she is driven by hatred to destroy the reputation of her rapist - she is not allowed to tell others what happened to her!

There are many other situations which seem puzzling but become clear once the question is asked - are you focusing on the net spiritual consequences or on stopping suffering? In fact both views are viable Jewish views. The distinguishing factor is whether the focus is on saving the person or on saving him for the proper motivation.

An additional issue of theological lens is how does one look at someone in need? Do you say this person needs my help and if I don't help him he will suffer? Or do I say, "It is a mitzva to help people but if I don't help then someone else will since G-d determines whether a person suffers or not. Even if I refuse to help all it means is that I lose the merit of helping another person."

This is a dispute in Bava Metzia (83b) as to whether man needs to take action against injustice and crime – when the Torah parameters don't help. The Meiri says that one can not use methods which were not permitted by the Torah and therefore it is G-d's job to solve the problems. The Rashba and others say that one must use techniques that work – even if they don't conform to the prescriptions of the Torah. Man must do something.

Excessive fear of sinning prevents helping

One of the significant contributing factors in child abuse in Orthodox community is that the rabbinical authorities of the community have succeeded very well in teaching the extreme dangers of three sins – lashon harah, informing and chilul hashem. An additional factor is the complexity of halachic understanding – these issues can not be decided by a laymen, or even the average rabbi but only a gadol (world class rabbi) is competent to decide what is permitted in these cases. Thus people are terrified of reporting rumors of child abuse or even actual child abuse because of the possibility of speaking lashon harah. They are afraid of losing their portion in the World to Come by reporting abuse. They are fully aware of the reality of the spiritual poison which is generated every time they open their mouth and speak even doubtful lashon harah. They have been exquisitely sensitized to possibility of harm the family of the alleged perpetrator. They are well aware of the dangers of chillul hashem if word gets out of a Jewish molester. They know exactly how they and their family will be shunned for being an informer. They know that their children and that of the molester will be unable to get proper shiduchim for their children.

The awareness of the severe consequences for erring in these matters is greatly complicated by the Chofetz Chaim's widely accepted approach of concern for the views of all authorities and the desirability of behavior which satisfies apparently conflicting views. Thus prior to the Chofetz Chaim's monumental work of the sin of lashon harah – the major authorities such as the Rambam simple said not to say bad or harmful things about others. Prior to the Chofetz Chaim it was assumed that lashon harah was a matter of social sensitivity and concern for others. The Chofetz Chaim showed that the issue was not simple and he collected in encyclopedic manner the concerns and subtle issues from a wide range of halachic sources and medrashim. In fact that which the Chofetz Chaim wrote hundreds of pages of sources and analysis was described by the Rambam (Hilchos De'os 7:1-6): in six brief paragraphs.

Fear of these three sins creates a formidable barrier to taking action and therefore it is not very likely that a religious Jew would take the initiative to report a molester to the police. It is also severely diminishes the chance that he will even report his/her concerns or even actually be abuse to parents, principal or rabbi. Even if he does, the

Child & Domestic Abuse

rabbi is likely to also be concerned with all the above and avoid doing anything other than warning that this should not be talked about or reported to the police.

People ask – what is wrong with fearing sin? What is wrong with being concerned with the reputation of the Jewish people or one's community or even the reputation of those with in it? The problem is that the Torah mandates in no uncertain terms that we are required to protect others. Thus the Torah isn't just a collection of prohibitions against actions. Rather it is a dynamic collection of what should be done which are combined with concerns for refrain from action. By being strongly focused on not doing something wrong – you increase the likelihood of not doing something good.

This dialectic between avoiding bad and yet doing go is illustrated by the very verse which prohibits lashon harah. The full verse (Vayikra 19:16) states, "You shall not go around spreading gossip amongst your people nor shall you stand idly by the blood of your fellow man – I am the L-rd." In other words the Torah itself makes the prohibition of lashon harah conditional on whether the speech benefits another person. Thus saying negative things about another is a mitzva when it is beneficial (to'eles).

So it is with chilul hashem (profaning G-d's name). The consideration of whether reporting abuse will cause chilul Hashem must take into a account the chilul hashem that results from doing nothing to protect the children and correct abuse and stop harm. Or alternatively the chilul hashem resulting from dealing with abuse must be weighed with the kiddush hashem (sanctifying G-d's name) that results when the world sees how the children are being protected against abuse).

Even reporting is a balancing act. The prohibition of informing is not to gratuitously place a Jew in the hands of secular authorities where he and his money will be harmed. However the halacha is clear that this is permitted when that person is a threat to the community or even an individual. The second part - the necessity of informing to protect another person - is ignored because of the awareness of the strong prohibition of informing on a Jew

Excessive fear of sinning prevents helping

Thus there are in fact legitimate reasons for inaction because of the serious possibility of doing something wrong with horrible consequences. "Why take the chance of saying or doing something that is prohibited and produce irreparable damage to yourself and others?"

However, while that is unquestionable true – the inaction is itself dangerous and one faces serious consequences for failure to protect others from harm. Thus inaction is not the safe and prudent path as it is typically viewed. There is no escaping of the requirement to act – even if there is danger of erring. Both action and inaction must be weighted and considered.

Mesilas Yeshorim (Chapter 20): It is important to understand that one should not view an act of piety according to its initial consequences but he should examine and think about also the long-term consequences. That is because an action might initially look good but according to its consequences it is bad – so therefore he should avoid it. If he does it anyway, he is a sinner not a pious person. For example consider the incident with Gedalial ben Achichem. It is clear to us that because of his great piety he did not judge Yishmael for the bad and did not accept lashon harah…. The consequences were that he was killed and the Jewish people were dispersed in exile and the flicker of hope that remained – was extinguished. In fact the people that were killed as a result of his actions have been described as if he personally killed them. … We also find that the Second Temple was destroyed because of this type of unthinking piety. This was the incident of Bar Kamtza. It says in Gittin (56a) that the Rabbis thought that they should offer the blemished animal as a sacrifice. But R' Zechariya ben Avkulas told them that they could not - because people would say that it is permissible to sacrifice a blemished animal. They said so we should kill this animal so it can't be sacrificed. He replied that people will mistakenly think whenever a blemish is found in a sanctified animal it should be killed. Thus the animal was not sacrificed and the informer went to the Roman government and told them that the Jews refused to offer the sacrifice. The Emperor came and destroyed Jerusalem. Thus the gemora concludes, "Because of the humility of R' Zechariya, Jerusalem and the Temple were destroyed and the Jews were sent in to Exile." Thus we should not judge an act of piety solely by itself. We need to examine it carefully from all the perspectives that a person can think of until he judges it truly as to whether doing the deed is preferable to not doing it…

Child & Domestic Abuse

Rav Chaim Shmuelevitz (Sichos Musar #33 5731): Everyone is required to thoroughly examine his deeds especially before Rosh HaShanna - the Day of Judgment. This obligation is not just to discover transgressions and lapses in observance of the commands. It also includes the evaluation whether one's path in serving G-d is the correct one for him since everyone has a unique path. The issue of Avodas HaShem is such that a person could keep all the mitzvos yet have a completely false approach to serving G-d. The problem is compounded by the fact that he might have incorrectly assumed that what he was doing would be pleasing to G-d. Nevertheless all his efforts would have been to accomplish a mistaken goal. Consequently if he has not carefully evaluated the correctness of his plan then all his efforts and sacrifices are wasted. Furthermore he is punished according to the degree of effort he made to accomplish this wrong plan. This can be seen from the fact that Rav Yochanon ben Zakkai who was not only the leading Torah scholar of his time but also had succeeded in saving Torah for all future generations was frightened before his death. He cried before his students and said, "I see before me two paths - one to Gan Eden and the other to Gehinom and I don't know where they are taking me. Shouldn't I cry?" His fear was not because of failing to keep the whole Torah. His fear was solely because he might have failed to properly have done his Avodas HaShem. There is the additional problem with Avodas HaShem - that one simply can't repent for doing it incorrectly since it is easy to be mistaken and assume that you are doing the right thing.

Mishna Berura (Shaar HaTziyun 622:6): A person many times despairs of correcting his faults and concludes that if G-d decrees that he dies because of his failure there is nothing he can do about it. However this is a mistaken attitude because in the end, G-d will get the correction of the soul that He wants. The soul will be reincarnated over and over again into this world until the correction is achieved. Consequently why should the soul repeatedly suffer death and the anguish of the grave and other things? Proof of this is from Yonah whom G-d wanted to prophesize for Nineveh and he tried to escape to the sea where prophecy does not occur. We see that he sunk into sea and was swallowed by the great fish and was in its belly many days where it seems that it was impossible to fulfill G-d's command. Nevertheless we see that at the end G-d's will was fulfilled and he went and prophesized. Thus it is with everyman according to his Divinely ordained task. Therefore as it says in Avos (4:22): Don't view the grave as a refuge—because you were born against your will,

Excessive fear of sinning prevents helping

you live against your will, you die against your will and against your will you will have to justify all your actions to the Heavenly court.

Child & Domestic Abuse

G-d's reasons for rape and abuse

Perhaps the most difficult issue for a religious Jew to face is why did it happen? Since we know that nothing happens without G-d's approval - that must mean that He wanted the abuse to happen. There are in fact in two alternative views which need to be considered. Strangely enough each approach is legitimate within Torah sources but only one is comforting and the other is viewed as distressing. Which is which is dependent on the individual and his/her psychological and spiritual attitude.

The first approach, which is the dominant one today, is the G-d centered view that G-d is responsible for all events and He wanted it to happen. Even if a leaf falls off a tree is was caused by Divine Providence. There are a number of reasons why G-d wanted to suffering to happen. 1) Because the need for atonement – either in this lifetime or for a previous existence. The Ramban states that without the concept of reincarnation (gilgul) it is impossible to understand the suffering of the righteous and innocent. Thus most suffering is the result of sin. 2) The need for testing and character refinement through adversity. Thus the suffering is not the result of sin but is the means of getting greater personal growth and reward in the world to come. 3) Suffering of love is simply n order to give greater reward in the World to Come. This view is found comforting because everything has meaning and the main test is to accept that the suffering is G-d's will. The suffering is pre-ordained and thus there is no protection against it. The only way to prevent the suffering is to take the initiative to raise ones spiritual level so that there is no need for the suffering. If the desired consequences can be achieved by one's spiritual initiative then there is no need for the suffering. The perpetrator still needs to be punished because if he weren't wicked he would not have been selected to be the agent of the suffering. The concern that G-d is doing something cruel is answered simply by the statement that G-d is obviously is kind but we don't understand it and must accept whatever He does as kind. G-d is like a doctor who causes pain by amputating a limb or give chemo- therapy to save the person.

G-d's reasons for rape and abuse

The second approach is the man centered view that while G-d in fact runs the world – but He gives man free-will to do what he wants. Thus a man can hurt or kill another – even though G-d doesn't want it to happen – because of the granting of free-will. Consequently one can in fact prevent the harm from happening by human efforts. The Rambam explains that Divine Providence is reserved for those truly close to G-d and even a distraction from thinking about G-d makes you vulnerable to harm. The Netziv cites a Zohar as the source of this understanding. Rav Dessler cites Seforno that most Jews are not operating under Divine Providence. This is generally the approach found in the Rishonim and was the dominant approach until Chassidim introduced the first view about 150 years ago. This man centered view is comforting because G-d is not being cruel in any sense of the word. Rather it is man that causes suffering or the impersonal forces of chance or mazel. This approach puts the responsibility on man to act and to stop the suffering. It also means that one needs to focus on how he responds on a human level because not all efforts will be effective in stopping the harm. The first approach is much more fatalistic because ultimately one needs only accept what has happened and that it needed to happen.

The following is an illustration of the impact of theological lenses. A young lady once came to me for a theological consultation. This poised cheerful woman told me that when she was 10 she had been raped by two young yeshiva students at a religious summer camp. As a result of this incident she went into severe depression, became suicidal, and was finally placed in a mental hospital for an extended time. She said that baruch hashem, she had recovered and was no longer depressed or obsessed with revenge. Her visit was precipitated by having just seen her assailants walking down the street in Geula in Jerusalem with their wives and children - as if they had never done anything evil. She said there was only one issue left from her experience which she couldn't come to grips with - Why did G-d want her to be raped?" All the rabbis she had consulted with told her that it was G-d's will and that while they couldn't explain it that it must have been good and necessary. She just had to accept it as G-d's will. Her problem was that she couldn't accept that she worshipped a G-d that wanted this horrible thing to happen. I answered her that she was being told the dominant chassidic/kabbalistic view. However I told her that the Rishonim had a different view, i.e., that it is possible for a man to chose to hurt another - even though G-d doesn't want it to happen. That she will be compensated in the Next World for her suffering but that G-d didn't cause it to happen. She was able to accept that view.

Child & Domestic Abuse

If you focus on the net spiritual gain of an event - it is not hard to ignore human suffering. After all there is a reason that the person is suffering. The Ramchal says not to pray to stop your suffering. He says that it is equivalent to pay a surgeon not to do a lifesaving operation. G-d he says is the ultimate doctor and has prescribed this suffering for your own good. Why would you want to stop it? If the sufferer only accepted his situation he gets tremendous spiritual reward. On the other hand if you focus on the Torah command of "don't stand idly by the blood of your fellow" and "love your fellow as yourself" then it is critical to not only stop suffering but prevent it.

My point is that both views are totally legitimate Torah views but they lead to strongly divergent actions towards suffering. What I am saying is not really a chiddush - everybody knows these things as the Mesilas Yeshorim says - but they are not aware of the consequences on our families and communities.

A final point is that there is an inverse relationship between maximizing the spiritual content of the universe and yashrus. The Malbim says that yashrus is taking the straight path from point A to B. If you don't see the events as they are but reinterpret them through theology lenses - that might be a true interpretation but it is not yashar. Similarly that while both pshat and derash are true - but derash is not pshat. The immediacy of outrage at suffering and desire to help is numbed by the indirect path and indirect nature of perceptions. This is probably also related to the kabalistic dispute as to whether tzimtzum - the original creation - was literally true or only figuratively. Is the world real or is it some illusionary video game?

Kiruv can be dangerous to marriage

There was a very well known kiruv personality. Perhaps you could say that he was a poster boy for kiruv. Warm and wise and very articulate in expressing the wisdom of the Torah. He was much in demand as a speaker - and as a consequence he spent much time flying between speaking engagement. Wherever he went he brought the light of Torah. It warmed his heart to see all the people he was influencing and he was a role model of humility and service of G-d. One day he was flying the long and boring stretch across the Atlantic when the stewardess asked him if he needed anything. He suspected that she might be Jewish so he engaged her in light banter – hoping to influence her to become more religiously observant. He stated in a joking tone that he was an outreach rabbi and that she probably should avoid him since he was a fundamentalist ultra-orthodox rabbi. She had never met such a charming and intelligent religious fanatic so she decided to play along. It turns out she wasn't Jewish - but she really enjoyed the discussion. The conversation deepened and she was really taken with this man. There was something about him that was different than all the men she had ever met. He of course told himself that he was motivated solely by altruistic reasons. The fact that she was stunningly beautiful and was quite intelligent and asked really good questions – simply made it a more interesting challenge. By the end of the flight they exchanged phone numbers and promised to stay in contact.

To make a long story short - he realized that she really made him feel alive. It was a wondrous thing watching her come up with a really deep question about the Ramchal that he had told her and the joy on her face when he took the question and connected it with Chassidic stories and Kabbala. It was an amazing thing realizing how much this beautiful woman benefited from everything he said. He realized that he once had that relationship with his wife of 20 years - but they hadn't had a deeper issue than who was coming for Shabbos - for at least 10 years. Besides his wife wasn't so beautiful anymore.

After much soul searching he realized that for the sake of his spirituality and hers he needed to drop his wife and marry her. The stewardess had readily agreed to convert -

Child & Domestic Abuse

to marry him. Nonetheless it wasn't easy breaking his wife's heart and destroying his kids - but he was willing to make the sacrifice for the sake of G-d. After all isn't spiritual growth the prime value? Besides all his wife could do was have babies and keep house. His interaction with this stewardess pushed him to spiritual heights and understanding. He just couldn't believe the profound Torah insights coming out of his mouth when he spoke with her. He decided he would abandon his family. He was young enough to start over again with a new family.

He did in fact divorce his wife, the stewardess converted and they married. Of course his former wife, family and community were totally devastated. But he moved elsewhere and is happily starting life over again with his beautiful student – purely for the sake of Heaven of course.

Abused wife's salvation: Waiting for a traffic light

Retelling a story of Dr. Naomi Remen

From a lecture at University of California June, 2008

. http://www.youtube.com/watch?v=Q1xBjlHEhtg

I know a woman who is an expert on wife abuse. She has helped many women by her lectures and her programs. I once met with her for dinner and I expressed my astonishment that such a gentle and delicate woman was so involved and knowledgeable about such a violent and unpleasant topic. She shocked me when she replied; "I was once an abused wife. My husband was a controlling and physically abusive person. However this was only in private. In public he was very sensitive. He was a respected and admired member of the community. Many envied me for what they thought was my marriage to an ideal husband. However I suffered a greater damage than the physical abuse – I completely lost my self-esteem. My husband succeeded – like many abusive husbands - in convincing me that I was stupid and incompetent and that his abuse of me was my fault. My whole existence became focused on trying to please him and finally get something right so I would not make him angry with me. Over the seven years of our marriage I lost all my self-esteem and became totally subordinate to his wishes and views of things. This all changed in a chance encounter with a total stranger in the few moments while I was waiting with my husband for the traffic light to change. I commented to my husband that the building across the street was a beautiful example of Art Deco architecture. He responded in the harsh belittling fashion he did when we were alone together. He condescendingly sneered that I had made a really stupid comment and there was nothing special about that building. However a stranger standing next to us rebuked him and told him that he was a real idiot because it was quite obvious that I was right. The traffic light turned green and the stranger walked away. But her comment had aroused something in me. It validated that I was an intelligent human being and that my husband was being abusive. That chance encounter started the restoration of my

Child & Domestic Abuse

dignity and self-esteem and gave me the strength and motivation to divorce my husband.

Lashon harah is sometimes a mitzva

Pischei Tshuva[1]**(O.C. 156):** I want to note here that while all the books of mussar are greatly concerned about the sin of lashon harah, I am greatly concerned about the opposite problem. I want to protest about the even greater and more common sin of refraining from speaking negatively when it is necessary to save someone from being harmed. For example if you saw a person waiting in ambush to kill someone or breaking into someone's house or store at night. Is it conceivable that you would refrain from notifying the intended victim to protect himself from the assailant - because of the prohibition of speaking lashon harah? By not saying anything you commit the unbearable sin of transgressing the prohibition of Vayikra (19:16): Do not speak lashon harah [but] do not stand idly by when the blood of your fellow man is threatened? By not speaking up, you violate the mitzva of returning that which is lost to its owner Devarim (22:2). Now if you can understand the obvious necessity of speaking up in these cases then what is the difference between a robber breaking into someone's house or store or seeing that his servants are secretly stealing from him or that his partner is deceiving him in their business or that another person is cheating him in commerce or that he is lending money to someone that you know doesn't repay? How is this different from stopping a proposed marriage to someone you know is a wicked person who would be a horrible husband. Saving a person from these situations is clearly included in the command (Devarim 22:2) to return to the person himself or his money. From where do we get the mistaken idea that in the case of murder, I will speak up but that it is prohibited to say anything in other situations where someone is being harmed? The general principle is that these are matters which depend upon the speakers motivation. If the informant's intent in relating these matters is entirely to cause harm that is lashon harah. However if his intent is to bring about benefit to the other person and to save him and to protect him – then it is a great mitzva. In my opinion this is the underlying intent of the Yerushalmi which the Magen Avraham brings which says that it is permitted to speak lashon harah about people who cause disputes. … [SEE RABBINIC SOURCES]

Nida[2]**(61a):** It was taught: That was the pit in which Yishmael ben Nesaniah filled with the bodies of the dead. As it is written (Yermiyahu 41:9): The pit which

Child & Domestic Abuse

Yishmael threw the bodies of the men he had killed by the hand of Gedaliah. But did Gedaliya in fact kill them? Didn't Yishmael kill them? But since Gedaliya should have been concerned with the advice of Yochanon ben Koreach and didn't do so he was regarded as if he killed them. Rava said that while one can't accept as true unsubstantiated lashon harah but you can act to protect yourself.

*Wife beating is always prohibited

Gra[3](Shulchan Aruch E.H. 154:9): If he habitually beats her cut off his hand – as it says in Sanhedrin (58b) that Rav Huna cut off the hand of someone who habitually hit others – and surely if the victim is his own wife.

Ohr Zarua[4](Bava Kama #161): ... It is prohibited for a man to beat his wife and furthermore if he does he must be for all the damage if she was hurt. If he regularly beats her and embarrasses her in public we force him to divorce her...

Rabbeinu Simcha[5](Beis Yosef E.H 154:3): (2) It is an accepted view that when a husband beats his wife it is a more severe crime then when he beats his fellow man. That is because there is no obligation to honor his fellow man while concerning his wife he is commanded to honor her more than he honors himself (Yevamos 62b). A person who beats his wife is to be placed in cherem and ostracized as well as flogged and punished with all manner of punished even to the point of cutting off his hand if he constantly beats her (Sanhedrin 58b). If she wants to get out of the marriage he should give her a divorce and she receives her kesuba. An attempt should be made to make peace between them but if he doesn't comply and continues to beat her and degrade her he should be excommunicated and forced by the secular government to divorce her or be forced to comply with whatever the Jewish authorities tell him (Gittin 88b)...

Rambam[6](Hilchos Chovel u'Mazik 4:16): If a man beats his wife he must pay her immediately for all the damage, suffering and all her embarrassment and the husband derives no benefit from the payment. If she wants to give the money to someone else she can give it. This is the ruling of the Gaonim [who were stricter than the Tosefta in that the husband no longer receives any benefit from the payment]. Furthermore her husband must pay for her medical treatment as he does for any other sickness.

Rema[7](E.H. 154:3): And similarly a man who habitually angry and frequently sends his wife out of the house. In such a case he is forced to divorce her because since he sometimes doesn't feed her and he does not fulfill his obligation to provide sexual relations – he is a rebel (mored) concerning both food and sex (Rashba 693). A

Child & Domestic Abuse

man who hits his wife has committed a sin just as if he had hit any other Jew. If he habitually hits her, the court should punish him, ostracize him and to beat him with all types of force as well as to make him take an oath that he will not do it anymore. If he doesn't obey the court – some say that he should be forced to divorce her. However this is only if he is first warned once or twice. That is because it is not normal for Jews to hit their wives – it is what the idolaters do. However this is only when he attacks her. However if she curses him without cause or ridicules his parents and he chastises her and she refuses to stop – some say that it is permitted to hit her while others says that even a bad wife can not be hit. The halacha is accord with the first opinion that she can be hit. If it is known who started the fight, the husband is not believed to say that she initiated. That is because all women are presumed to be righteous. Therefore observers need to be placed with them to see who is the cause of the problem. If she in fact cursed him without cause – she is to be divorced and not receive her kesuba. It seems to me that this is only if she habitually curses him without cause and only after she has been warned as we explained in 115. If she leaves his house and borrows money to eat – if she left because of constant beatings – he is obligated to pay for her expenses…

Prison is a legitimate punishment

Appropriate punishment

Ezra[8](7:26): Let judgment be executed on him with all diligence whether it be to execute him, to uproot him, or monetary punishment or imprisonment

Minchas Yitzchok[9](8:148): … it is obvious that someone who drives at excessive speeds and thus cannot stop quickly enough when needed without causing an accident - has the status of a rodef (pursuer) even if his behavior was much less serious. … If after warning him he continues to act in this way, it is permitted to report him to the police. It is obvious that this is true for the other behaviors mentioned such as stopping at stop signs which enable pedestrians to cross the street or if he is dangerously tailgating the car in front of him. The same applies if he is driving without a license – all of these are in the category of rodef which endangers himself and others. Even if he doesn't intend to endanger others he is still considered a rodef. Also included is if he stops his car in a way that endangers pedestrians or by parking on the sidewalk which forces the pedestrians to go into the street or any of the other ways that that are described in the letter. All of these are equivalent to digging a pit in the public area…

Mo'ed Koton[10](16a): From where do we derive that one may place lawbreakers in chains, put in prison and prosecute them? Ezra (7:26) said: Let judgment be executed on him with all diligence whether it be to execute him, to uproot him, or monetary punishment or imprisonment.

Rav Moshe Halberstam[11](Yeschurun 15 page 646): Let's return to the original question concerning a wicked molester whose evil inclination forces him to sin and be wicked and it is possible to turn him over to the government in order that he be incarcerated in prison for a number of years until he calms done and returns to G-d wholeheartedly. According to the sources we discussed before it is clear that there is no sin or transgression in handing him over to the authorities. In fact the opposite is true – it is a mitzva because by doing so he is caused to stop from doing the disgusting deeds. In addition we know that the government will not execute him. Therefore the essence of his punishment is that he will be forced to dwell for a number of years in

Child & Domestic Abuse

prison. This will be beneficial to him in that they will assign him a psychologist or psychiatrist who will supervise him and his activities with a watchful eye. Perhaps he will be able to find a resolution of his torment by means of this treatment. So in such a case it is obvious that it is a good thing to save him and to save his family from his incestual attacks on them.

Rav Moshe Halberstam[12](Yeschurun 15 page 651): ... Nevertheless we can conclude that whoever strives to prevent the father or family members from sinning [by sexual abuse] in any manner that is necessary to succeed – even if it means imprisonment – it is considered that he is doing a mitzva. However this has to be done intelligently with commonsense and not fanfare and publicity etc., in order not to cause damage to the other family members. What sin have they done? This is like the worlds of Shlomo [Mishlei 11:2], "With discretion is wisdom."

Rav Moshe Halberstam[13](Yeschurun 15 page 649-650): ...Bottom line if it is known that a specific person is actually sinning with children now then it is obligatory to save him from his sin by reporting it immediately to the government authorities so that they lock him up in jail. He should be imprisoned for an extended period of time until his lusts get under control and in a manner that there is no question that he will not repeat his crime. But if he is not involved now in sin but it is known that he does such things – then it would be proper to give him a warning that if it becomes known or it is heard that that he even touches a part of the finger nail of one of these children then he will go to jail for a long time. But this warning is not a prerequisite at all - as noted in the Rema and Shach. Therefore when it is not possible to warn him then he can still contact the government authorities immediately as we discussed before.

Rambam[14](Hilchos Chovel u'Mazik 8:11): .... Similarly all those who distress the community and harm it – it is permitted to hand them over to the non-Jewish government to be beaten, imprisoned and punished. However if the person is only disturbing an individual and not the community – it is prohibited to hand him over. It is also prohibited to cause the loss of the property of the moser – even though it permitted to cause the death of the moser himself. That is because his property belongs to his heirs.

Rambam[15](Sanhedrin 24:8-9): A judge has the right to quarrel with an offender, to curse him, to hit him, to pull out his hair and to force him take an oath to attest that he did or didn't do something.... Similarly he has the fight to bind his hands and feet

Prison is a legitimate punishment

and to imprison him as well as to push to the ground as it says (Ezra 7:26), Let judgment be executed on him with all diligence whether it be to execute him, to uproot him or to confiscate his goods or imprison him.

Rav Eliashiv[16](Divrei Sinai page 45-46): ... See Panim Me'eros (2:155) concerning our issue in which someone found an open chest from which much was stolen. There is reasonable circumstantial evidence that one of the workers was the thief. He was asked whether it was permissible to inform the secular authorities and that this will lead to him to confess ... However at the end the Panim Me'eros concludes, "It is improper to turn a Jew over to secular authorities as our Sages say they will treat him like a trapped animal and there is concern that if he confesses they will kill him." From here it is clear that this ruling is not applicable in our times. Therefore it is permitted to turn to the police. However since you raise the concern that this will lead to a chilul hashem, I can't render an opinion concerning this since I don't know how to evaluate it and therefore the matter must be determined by your evaluation.

Rav Shlomo Zalman Auerbach[17](Ve'aleyhi lo Yuval, volume 2:113-114 from R' M Broyde's Informing on other's): R' Yehuda Goldreicht said: "I asked Rav Auerbach about a particular Jew who stole a large sum of money and he was caught by the police in America. He was sentenced to a number of years in prison in America. Was it proper to assist in the collection of money for him [we were speaking about a large sum of $200,000] in order to fulfill the mitzvah of pidyon shevuyim to have him released from prison? When Rav Auerbach heard this he stated "Pidyon shevuyim?! What is the mitzvah of pidyon shevuyim here? The mitzvah of redeeming captives is only when the goyim are grabbing Jews, irrationally, for no proper reason, and placing them in prison. According to what I [Rav Auerbach] know, in America they do not irrationally grab Jews in order to squeeze money from them. The Torah says "do not steal" and he stole money—on the contrary, it is good that he serve a prison sentence, so that he learns not to steal!"

Rav Yehuda Silman[18](Yeschurun volume 15 page 663): ... 2) Concerning reporting him to the secular authorities. If the circumstances are that it is sufficient to remove him from the job and there is no concern that he will continue attacking children, then that is what should be done and he should not be reported. 3) However if there is a concern that he will continue to molest children, then at least because of

Child & Domestic Abuse

the requirement to stop him from sinning it is permitted to report him even if he does not molest in a way that he transgresses actual Torah prohibitions and is therefore not considered a rodef. But since in our days prison is not considered life threatening it is permitted to cause him to be imprisoned. ... 6) However if the suspect is prepared to accept therapy that will make him better - such as psychotherapy, or chemicals which suppress his sex drive – if it seems to the dayan that he will do what he promised [and sometimes with appropriate supervision] then treatment is preferable to reporting him to the police. However even if the molester is given the alternative of treatment and supervision instead of jail - he needs to quit his job which involves contact with children. 7) Outside of Israel where secular law is relevant there are additional reasons to be lenient and allow reporting to the police. ...

Rav Sternbuch[19](**1:850**): ...That is why in fact the secular law that requires a skilled driver with a license is in fact a just and obvious law for the welfare of society and we are fully obligated to observe these laws. Anyone who treats these laws with contempt and disobeys them, we are concerned that such a person can come to kill and therefore he deserves serious punishment – even imprisonment. (See Tashbatz 3:168 regarding having non-Jews imprison a Jew as punishment and also Maharshdam C.M. 55.6). ...Therefore it would appear that if the person is considered a danger to society and since we can't punish him ourselves, he should be reported to the police – with the permission of beis din or the rabbi of the community. This is in fact a mitzva since it is saving the community from harm and possible death.[SEE RABBINIC SOURCES]

Steipler Rav (Within the Domain of Gedolei Torah Vol 2 page 557-560): ... When Rav Lorenz told the story to the Steipler Rav, the Steipler screamed, "A Jew who sins and repeats that sin, it is better that he be punished in this world and not – G-d forbid – in the World to Come." He explained, "The punishment in this world is minor compared to what happens in the World to Come. Furthermore if you succeed in stopping the jail sentence he will continue to repeatedly commit this crime. It is better that he receive his punishment and perhaps learn self-restraint...In addition if I give you permission and you testify for his benefit it is obvious that every newspaper and all the public media will publicize the matter and it will also be a chilul HaShem when he sins again…"

Prison is a legitimate punishment

Free harmful person from jail – redeem captive?

R' Moshe Halberstam[20](Yeschurun 15 page 651): An additional factor to what we have discussed is a question mentioned in Shevet HaLevi (4:124.3) whether it is appropriate to help free a well known thief who has begged that efforts be made to get him released from prison. Rav Wosner answers that since the thief's life is not in danger by being in prison there is no obligation to make efforts to free people like this. In my opinion it is not only not an obligation to try and free a person in these circumstances but in fact one who tries to free a thief from prison is actually committing a sin. Who says that he won't seek revenge for his imprisonment or at least return quickly to committing more crimes. Who can say that things will work out differently and that he will cease his crimes if he is freed? Therefore it is prohibited to make efforts for him and to listen to his plea to be freed… Nevertheless we can conclude that whoever strives to prevent the father or family members from sinning [by sexual abuse] in any manner that is necessary to succeed – even if it means imprisonment – it is considered that he is doing a mitzva. However this has to be done intelligently with commonsense and not fanfare and publicity etc., in order not to cause damage to the other family members. What sin have they done? This is like the worlds of Shlomo [Mishlei 11:2], "With discretion is wisdom."

Rav Shlomo Zalman Auerbach (Ve'aleyhi lo Yuval, volume 2:113-114 from R' M Broyde's Informing on other's): R' Yehuda Goldreicht said: "I asked Rav Auerbach about a particular Jew who stole a large sum of money and he was caught by the police in America. He was sentenced to a number of years in prison in America. Was it proper to assist in the collection of money for him [we were speaking about a large sum of $200,000] in order to fulfill the mitzvah of pidyon shevuyim to have him released from prison? When Rav Auerbach heard this he stated "Pidyon shevuyim?! What is the mitzvah of pidyon shevuyim here? The mitzvah of redeeming captives is only when the goyim are grabbing Jews, irrationally, for no proper reason, and placing them in prison. According to what I [Rav Auerbach] know, in America they do not irrationally grab Jews in order to squeeze money from them. The Torah says "do not steal" and he stole money—on the contrary, it is good that he serve a prison sentence, so that he learns not to steal!"

Shevet HaLevi[21](4:124.3): Concerning a well known thief who has stolen from many people and has harmed the public and now he his begging to be released from

Child & Domestic Abuse

jail. Is it properly to do that? ... From all these sources we see that there is no concern at all to have him remain in jail in order that he not harm others since his life is not in danger there. The Chovas Yair (139) says there is only a concern when jail is actually life threatening... My opinion is that as long as there is no danger to his life by being in jail, there is no obligation to make any efforts to free such people...

Today's prison are not considered life threatening

Rav Eliashiv[22](Divrei Sinai page 45-46): ...See Panim Me'eros (2:155) concerning our issue in which someone found an open chest from which much was stolen. There is reasonable circumstantial evidence that one of the workers was the thief. He was asked whether it was permissible to inform the secular authorities and that this will lead to him to confess ... However at the end the Panim Me'eros concludes, "It is improper to turn a Jew over to secular authorities as our Sages say they will treat him like a trapped animal and there is concern that if he confesses they will kill him." From here it is clear that this ruling is not applicable in our times. Therefore it is permitted to turn to the police.

Rav Moshe Halberstam[23](Yeschurun 15 page 651): An additional factor to what we have discussed is a question mentioned in Shevet HaLevi (4:124.3) whether it is appropriate to help free a well known thief who has begged that efforts be made to get him released from prison. Rav Wosner answers that since the thief's life is not in danger by being in prison there is no obligation to make efforts to free people like this. ...

Rav Yehuda Silman[24](Yeschurun volume 15 page 663): 2) Concerning reporting him to the secular authorities. If the circumstances are that it is sufficient to remove him from the job and there is no concern that he will continue attacking children, then that is what should be done and he should not be reported. 3) However if there is a concern that he will continue to molest children, then at least because of the requirement to stop him from sinning it is permitted to report him even if he does not molest in a way that he transgresses actual Torah prohibitions and is therefore not considered a rodef. But since in our days prison is not considered life threatening it is permitted to cause him to be imprisoned.

Shevet HaLevi[25](4:124.3): Concerning a well known thief who has stolen from many people and has harmed the public and now he his begging to be released from jail. Is it properly to do that? ... From all these sources we see that there is no concern

Prison is a legitimate punishment

at all to have him remain in jail in order that he not harm others since his life is not in danger there. The Chovas Yair (139) says there is only a concern when jail is actually life threatening… My opinion is that as long as there is no danger to his life by being in jail, there is no obligation to make any efforts to free such people…

Child & Domestic Abuse

Self-defense against uncertain danger (rodef)

Rav Yehuda Silman[26]**(Yeschurun 15):** Question: Is it permitted to kill someone that there are doubts whether he is in fact a rodef (threat to life)? I was asked concerning a security guard in a public place e.g., the entrance of a restaurant or a mall who notices a man approach and he appears suspicious. The person is acting strangely and appears to be an Arab. When the security guard approaches him, he begins to run. The security guards suspects that he is a terrorist. This is only a suspicion since it is possible that he is in fact a Jew and there are people in the world who act strangely. In addition it is possible that the suspicious stranger is running away simply out of panic. However it is possible that in a short time the stranger will in fact cause a serious terror attack. Is it permitted to kill the stranger when the facts are not clear? This is a common question and a similar question can be asked regarding a bank teller who is suddenly confronted with a bandit with a pistol in his hand. There are many times when it is later determined that the gun was only a toy and even if it were real the bandit didn't intend to kill but only to scare the bank teller. Nevetheless there is a doubt whether the person is in danger. In such circumstances is it permitted to kill him? Answer:... Conclusions: 1) It appears that we hold in practice that it is permitted to killed a suspected rodef. In other words someone who is doing actives that endanger others even if there are doubts. ... 4) Therefore in the two versions of the question that were asked concerning a suspicious person it is permitted to kill him. That is only in a case there are valid bases to suspect that he is trying to kill. 5) In contrast in the case of someone running in the forest or is shooting and there are doubts as to his intent[- he is not to be viewed as a rodef because we assume he has a legitimate reason for doing these things (chezkas kashrus).

Responsa & comments of Gedolim

Chasam Sofer (Gittin 7a) – Harassment

Chasam Sofer[27](Gittin 7a): Mar Ukva said that there are people who are irritating me [verbal – Rashi]. ... Even though it was only verbal abuse, nevertheless if it wasn't for the fact that Mar Ukva could save himself from this abuse by arising early and going to the study hall - it would seem that he would have been allowed to report his abusers to the government... We see from Rashi's explanation that it was clear that if Mar Ukva had been abused monetarily or by forgery he would have been permitted to report his abusers to the government and he would not have been required to go to the study hall. That is simply because if a person comes to kill you than you have every right to kill them first. This is also the ruling of the Rambam (Hilchos Chovel u'Mazik 9:11): "And similarly if a person abuses and harasses the community it is permitted to give him over to the secular government to be beaten... In contrast if only an individual is being harassed it is prohibited to report him..." This would indicate that the Rambam is referring to verbal harassment. Therefore if the assailant caused an actual loss it would be permitted to report him to the government so that he doesn't cause further loss. This is the ruling of the Rema (C.M. 388:9) and it is also the ruling of the Shach (C.M. 388:59-60). However while it seems obvious to the Rambam that if one verbal harasses a community it is permitted to report him to the government – the commentaries don't show the sources of this ruling. It must be that this ruling is learned from this gemora. It would seem that if hadn't been for the fact that Mar Ukva had a solution to the harassment problem by going to the study hall it would have been permitted to report his assailants to the secular government. However this solution is only relevant for an individual. But it is not relevant for the community and therefore it is clearly permitted to report the community nuisance to the government. Also see the Pnei Yehoshua's discussion of this gemora where he says that the solution of going to the study hall and complaining to G-d about the assailant is not correct if one can stop the harasser in other ways. However he says if the harassers cause him to waste time from Torah and prayer because of his upset he can stop the harassers in any manner...

Child & Domestic Abuse

Pischei Teshuva – lashon harah

Pischei Tshuva[28](O.C. 156): I want to note here that while all the books of mussar are greatly concerned about the sin of lashon harah, I am greatly concerned about the opposite problem. I want to protest about the even greater and more common sin of refraining from speaking negatively when it is necessary to save someone from being harmed. For example if you saw a person waiting in ambush to kill someone or breaking into someone's house or store at night. Is it conceivable that you would refrain from notifying the intended victim to protect himself from the assailant - because of the prohibition of speaking lashon harah? By not saying anything you commit the unbearable sin of transgressing the prohibition of Vayikra (19:16): Do not speak lashon harah [but] do not stand idly by when the blood of your fellow man is threatened? By not speaking up, you violate the mitzva of returning that which is lost to its owner Devarim (22:2). Now if you can understand the obvious necessity of speaking up in these cases then what is the difference between a robber breaking into someone's house or store or seeing that his servants are secretly stealing from him or that his partner is deceiving him in their business or that another person is cheating him in commerce or that he is lending money to someone that you know doesn't repay? How is this different from stopping a proposed marriage to someone you know is a wicked person who would be a horrible husband. Saving a person from these situations is clearly included in the command (Devarim 22:2) to return to the person himself or his money. From where do we get the mistaken idea that in the case of murder, I will speak up but that it is prohibited to say anything in other situations where someone is being harmed? The general principle is that these are matters which depend upon the speaker's motivation. If the informant's intent in relating these matters is entirely to cause harm that is lashon harah. However if his intent is to bring about benefit to the other person and to save him and to protect him – then it is a great mitzva. In my opinion this is the underlying intent of the Yerushalmi which the Magen Avraham brings which says that it is permitted to speak lashon harah about people who cause disputes. ... It is obvious that even concerning those who cause disputes it is not permitted to speak lashon harah gratuitously about them in all matters. It is only permitted for those things directly related to the particular dispute. It is only permitted concerning that which they are trying to harm others. In such a case it is permitted to reveal degrading things about them in order to save others. ... Unfortunately I have seen many times where someone witnesses another person trying

Responsa & comments of Gedolim

to cause harm to someone – and he suppresses the information and says, "Why should I get involved in a matter which isn't my business…However one needs to be very careful about these and similar matters. Our Sages have said – when the permissibility depends on motivation - it says, "And you should be afraid of your G-d."

Rambam – Damage to a community

Rambam[29](**Hilchos Sanhedrin 2:12**): A person can carry out his own judgments if he has the power. Since he is acting strictly in accordance with the religion and the halacha he is not obligated to exert himself to go to the Jewish court. This is true even though he suffers no monetary loss if we waited to first go to the Jewish court. Therefore if afterwards his opponent agrees to court and the judges determine that he has acted properly according to the halacha and that his judgment is true – they don't abrogate the judgment he made himself.

Rambam[30](**Hilchos Chovel uMazik 8:9**): It is prohibited to hand over a Jew to non-Jews – whether it is the Jew himself or his money. It prohibited even if the Jew is a wicked person and even if he harasses him and causes him great aggravation. Who ever does hand over a Jew to non-Jews – whether it is physically or financially – does not have a portion in the World to Come.

Rambam[31](**Hilchos Chovel uMazik 8:11**): …Similarly all those who distress the community and harm it – it is permitted to hand them over to the non-Jewish government to be beaten, imprisoned and punished. However if the person is only disturbing an individual and not the community – it is prohibited to hand him over. It is also prohibited to cause the loss of the property of the moser – even though it permitted to cause the death of the moser himself. That is because his property belongs to his heirs.

Rav Moshe Sternbuch – dangerous driver

Rav Moshe Sternbuch[32](**1:850**): Question: A Jewish driver who normal speeds or doesn't have a license – is it permitted to report him to the police? Answer: It states explicitly in Shulchan Aruch (Y.D. 388:12) that if someone is engaged in counterfeiting and is thus a danger to the community – he should be warned to stop. If he doesn't listen to the warning it is possible to report him to the police. The Gra there says that the counterfeiter has the status of a rodef (pursuer) even though he does not intend to harm others and even though the harm is an indirect result of his actions and

Child & Domestic Abuse

even though the danger is only a possibility not a certainty. There is nothing more dangerous than a reckless driver who is speeding or one who has no knowledge of proper driving skills - as indicated by the fact he has no license. Such people are likely to kill other, chas v'shalom and therefore they have the halachic status of rodef (pursuer). That is why in fact the secular law that requires a skilled driver with a license is in fact a just and obvious law for the welfare of society and we are fully obligated to observe these laws. Anyone who treats these laws with contempt and disobeys them, we are concerned that such a person can come to kill and therefore he deserves serious punishment – even imprisonment. (See Tashbatz 3:168 regarding having non-Jews imprison a Jew as punishment and also Maharshdam C.M. 55.6). However it is appropriate not to hand him over to the government immediately but only after he has been warned first by the rav of the community or the beis din. They should tell him that if he continues violating traffic laws they will report him to the police so that he will be punished appropriately. (It should be done this way because if he is simply warned he will not believe that he will be reported to the police.). If despite the warning he insists of violating traffic laws and showing contempt for the community he should be reported. (R' Yaakov Kaniefsky was very angry with those who violated traffic laws whose purpose is to protect the lives of the members of society. I heard that someone once came to him because he was worried that he was about to receive a very severe punishment because he had violated the traffic laws. He wanted to receive a beracha that he would be free of the punishment. R' Kaniefsky replied with a very sharp admonition and told him that in truth he deserved to be punished!) (This was even though R' Kaniefsky was not necessarily in agreement with the secular laws in general). Therefore it would appear that if the person is considered a danger to society and since we can't punish him ourselves, he should be reported to the police – with the permission of beis din or the rabbi of the community. This is in fact a mitzva since it is saving the community from harm and possible death.

Rav Moshe Sternbuch[33]**(5:398):** I received his letter and I was very upset at the outrageous behavior of the principal who refused to listen to the claims against the teacher concerning alleged disgusting deeds – because he said it was lashon harah. Now the accusations against the teacher are increasing and the principal still stubbornly insists that there is not adequate evidence in the matter and therefore it is better to be concerned with the prohibition of lashon harah – then to investigate the matter. The assertions of the principal are total nonsense and they provide an opening

Responsa & comments of Gedolim

for destruction – G-d forbid. It is a fundamental obligation for a rosh yeshiva or principal to listen to all rumors and suspicions concerning that which occurs in his domain. That is because the first obligation he has is to guard the souls of his students. Therefore he has to be concerned with everything – even if it turns out to be a false alarm. So even though the teacher is presumed to be a good person – nevertheless whatever issues that are related to the protecting of the students – if there is even the slightest possibility that something might harm the children or young students – the principal is obligated to investigate to determine whether the suspicions are valid and/or to make a special effort to keep the suspected teacher under close observation. It is important to keep in mind that the essential prohibition of speaking or listening to lashon harah is when it is said by a person who is an enemy or is jealous of the person being talked about and thus his motivation is not pure. However when the negative information is from a person who has pure motivation it is necessarily to be concerned with each and every claim or rumor in order to prevent someone being harmed. A suspicion which is suppressed by the prohibition of lashon harah could possibly be critical knowledge that is need to prevent harm to many people. Once I was visiting the Gerrer Rebbe and he asked me about a certain young man. Since he was concerned that I might have objections about revealing the information because of lashon harah he said to me, "You should know that there is no prohibition of lashon harah in this house because everything spoken here is for a beneficial reason. And everything that I hear I use for beneficial purposes and with G-d's help it will always be done for a beneficial reason." I heard about the rabbinical conferences attended by the holy Chofetz Chaim who gave a talk about lashon harah. At the end he asked the rabbis that were present to sign a pledge to be careful from lashon harah. Rav Chaim Ozer refused to sign. There are various versions as to the reason for this. According to what I heard, he replied that the city rabbi has to know and listen to everything – even if there is just a remote possibility that it is true and to investigate whether the assertions and concerns are true. He was afraid that as a consequence of signing the document he would be more strict and more cautious regarding lashon harah than he should be - and that this would cause many to suffer. Therefore he felt that it was better that they make a decree to learn the halachos of lashon harah – than to agree never to speak or hear lashon harah. The bottom line is that it is an important mitzva to communicate every single suspicion and the principal needs to listen to each suspicion and to be concerned and to be careful to protect the students. If he is negligent in this matter he is included in the curse against those who do G-d's work in

Child & Domestic Abuse

a false way. Today there are many different types of opportunities to corrupt the youth and therefore it is necessary to be exceedingly careful in protecting these holy ones – the students who are engaged in studying G-d's Torah. (As is expressed by the Rambam at the end of Hilchos Shemita and Yovel).

Rav Shlomo Zalman Auerbach – child abuse

Rav S. Z. Auerbach[34](**Nishmas Avraham (4:208-211)**): A child or baby is brought to the hospital with signs of "battered child" syndrome i.e., with many fractures in his skull or body or internal bleeding because of blows or hard kicks or with severe burns either from electric or boiling water and the like that were done cruelly and intentionally by one or both of his parents. It is prohibited after the completion of treatment to return him to his house because then beatings would just continue until he died. Because of the real danger to his life, the doctor is obligated to notify the courts and then by means of a court order, the child will be transferred to a foster family or institution. It would seem that there is no prohibition of moser (informing) since we are dealing with a life threatening situation and the parents have the halachic status of rodef (pursuer). Therefore it is permitted to inform the authorities even if the child will automatically be removed from the parents and given to a family or institution which is not religious. However it is obvious that the beis din has to do whatever is in its power to try and ensure that the child is transferred to a family or institution which is observant And particularly in the Diaspora, the beis din has to be concerned that the child not be transferred to a non-Jewish family or institution. Rav Shlomo Zalman Auerbach agreed with me.

Rav Shmuel Wosner – dangerous driver

Rav Shmuel Wosner[35](**Shevet HaLevi 2:58**): 1) **Question:** Concerning someone who works for the tax department and he discovers someone cheating the government and is required by law to report it to the justice department. He wants to know whether he is considered an informer (moser) according to halacha or do we say that "the law of the land is the law" and thus he would not be an informer? **Answer:** Concerning the issues of taxes – there is no halachic authority who denies that this is included in the principle "the law of the land is the law." This is true even for those who disagree with the Rema (C.M. 369:8) as to the nature of "the law of the land is the law." See the Shach and Levush and the responsa Hashiv Moshe… Concerning the issue of reporting the tax cheat to the government see Bava Metzia (83b) concerning R'

Responsa & comments of Gedolim

Eliezer the son of Rav Shimon bar Yochai. The gemora reports that he reported thieves to the government. This is proof that where the government has authorized a Jew to report thieves that it is permitted. Even though he was criticized "how long are you handing the people of our G-d to be killed" – because the punishment for thieves in those days was death. This is relevant also for a similar criticism from Eliyahu Hanavi to R' Yishmael which is reported in that gemora. However the actual halacha seems that even when it results in the death penalty it is considered "the law of the land is the law." See the Ritva on that gemora which is found in the Shita Mekubetzes. The Be'er HaGola (C.M. 388) writes that it has already become accepted practice that the leaders of the community decreed there should not be any fraud or deception against the secular government. The community leaders have announced that it was permitted to publicize and reveal those men who were cheating the government. A person who wishes to escape paying taxes owed to the government and another Jew reveals this – this is not considered the crime of informing. Even though the Rema states that revealing this information is bad because it is like returning a lost object to a non-Jew – but that is only concerning an individual non-Jew. But that which is applicable to the government and the tax auditor was appointed to discover fraud – there is no prohibition in revealing the fraud. However it is best if a person should not work as a tax auditor which requires revealing this type of information. Even though revealing the information is permitted – it is not a pious thing to do as we see from the Yerushalmi. Also look at the Responsa of the Alshech who states that a person is not considered an informant for those things required by the law of the land….It is also obvious that this is not comparable to the case of R' Eleazar ben R' Shimon (Bava Metzia 83a) which involved danger to the person arrested. In contrast in our case here when they will just punish the person arrested and there is never a threat to life.

Rav Yehuda Silman – child abuse

Rav Yehuda Silman[36]**(Yeschurun 15):** Question: Is it permitted to kill someone that there are doubts whether he is in fact a rodef (threat to life)? I was asked concerning a security guard in a public place e.g., the entrance of a restaurant or a mall who notices a man approach and he appears suspicious. The person is acting strangely and appears to be an Arab. When the security guard approaches him, he begins to run. The security guards suspects that he is a terrorist. This is only a suspicion since it is possible that he is in fact a Jew and there are people in the world who act strangely. In addition it is possible that the suspicious stranger is running

Child & Domestic Abuse

away simply out of panic. However it is possible that in a short time the stranger will in fact cause a serious terror attack. Is it permitted to kill the stranger when the facts are not clear? This is a common question and a similar question can be asked regarding a bank teller who is suddenly confronted with a bandit with a pistol in his hand. There are many times when it is later determined that the gun was only a toy and even if it were real the bandit didn't intend to kill but only to scare the bank teller. Nevertheless there is a doubt whether the person is in danger. In such circumstances is it permitted to kill him? Answer:... Conclusions: 1) It appears that we hold in practice that it is permitted to killed a suspected rodef. In other words someone who is doing actives that endanger others even if there are doubts. ... 4) Therefore in the two versions of the question that were asked concerning a suspicious person it is permitted to kill him. That is only in a case there are valid bases to suspect that he is trying to kill. 5) In contrast in the case of someone running in the forest or is shooting and there are doubts as to his intent[- he is not to be viewed as a rodef because we assume he has a legitimate reason for doing these things (chezkas kashrus).

Rav Yehuda Silman[37](Yeschurun volume 15 page 662): 5) It is obvious in these matters of child abuse that it not necessary to have formal witnesses. As we see in Bava Metzia (83) that R' Eliezer bar R' Shimon had the Romans arrest those who were drinking in the tavern and were sleepy. ... The commentaries explain that the obvious reason for not needing witnesses but they could rely even on circumstantial evidence is because this was not a court procedure to punish wrongdoers. Rather it was either done to obey the law of the kingdom or it was to stop someone from sinning. The Rashba is cited in the Beis Yosef that witnesses are not needed in such a case...". That is because we are concerned only with the knowledge of truth in order to stop the harm and to make protective measures against iniquity. Furthermore according to what I said that even a doubtful rodef is permitted to be killed it is obvious that it is permitted for us to take protective action even if we have unresolved doubts.

Rav Yehuda Silman[38](Yeschurun volume 15 page 663): The laws that have emerged from our discussion concerning child molesters. We see that there are two separate issues 1) Concerning removing the perpetrator from his job. In this issue we establish that the halacha follows the view of the Sho'el u'Meishiv that it is enough that there are bad rumors and there is concern because of doubts. It seems that in such a case where there seems to be a basis for these rumors it is possible to remove him

Responsa & comments of Gedolim

from his job even in the middle of the year and he does not receive any compensation for the remainder of his contract or for loss of job. 2) Concerning reporting him to the secular authorities. If the circumstances are that it is sufficient to remove him from the job and there is no concern that he will continue attacking children, then that is what should be done and he should not be reported. 3) However if there is a concern that he will continue to molest children, then at least because of the requirement to stop him from sinning it is permitted to report him even if he does not molest in a way that he transgresses actual Torah prohibitions and is therefore not considered a rodef. But since in our days prison is not considered life threatening it is permitted to cause him to be imprisoned. 4) However the decision as to whether to report a molester is not given to everyone as the Yam Shel Shlomo said Rather it is given to a dayan or an important person. 5) Furthermore, the understanding of the facts of the situation as to what actions are needed can be based upon the evidence of children or any other evidence which arouses a serious question such as tape recordings, letters, or polygraph tests. In general without this - if there is no evidence even according to what is accepted by secular law – there can be no punishment. The point is that there is no requirement that the evidence must be valid according to the Torah. 6) However if the suspect is prepared to accept therapy that will make him better - such as psychotherapy, or chemicals which suppress his sex drive – if it seems to the dayan that he will do what he promised [and sometimes with appropriate supervision] then treatment is preferable to reporting him to the police. However even if the molester is given the alternative of treatment and supervision instead of jail - he needs to quit his job which involves contact with children. 7) Outside of Israel where secular law is relevant there are additional reasons to be lenient and allow reporting to the police. 8) It is a good idea to establish a dayan or a beis din to make the decisions about the above issues and therefore men should be selected for this purpose who are experienced in these matters because of the serious of the matter which requires special expertise.

Rav Yehuda Silman[39](Yeschurun 22 page 589-590): Is there an obligation for the molester to pay for psychotherapy? One major talmid chachom questioned whether psychotherapy is included in the payment for ripoi (cure). That is because he claims that we know from experience that those who are molested as children or as teenagers are rarely cured. He says that in the majority of cases the treatment that takes place over many years only helps to deal with the associated problems [and isn't

Child & Domestic Abuse

a cure]. I disagree with this position. The fact is that in a large percentage of cases there is fact full recovery and in almost all cases there is at least benefit from the therapy and thus it is obvious in my opinion that psychotherapy is included in the category of ripoi (cure). Consider the case of someone who was physically assaulted and there is no cure to his wounds and consequently he is required to have treatment for the rest of his life – would anyone seriously think that this treatment is not called ripoi (cure) – of course not!

This answer would seem to be relevant only for those e.g., Sephardim who follow the view of Rav Yosef Karo. He states in the Shulchan Aruch (C.M. 1:2) that the contemporary beis din judges and exacts payment for unemployment (sheves) and cure (ripoi). However this apparently is not applicable for those who follow the view of the Rema who rules that we don't judge and exact payment today in these matters. In fact there is no practical difference between the two positions. The Rema continues by saying, "We force the assailant to placate the victim and we fine him according to what is deemed appropriate by beis din as is explained in Shulchan Aruch(C.M. 1:5)." There the Shulchan Aruch states, "Even though judges who don't have semicha in Israel do not collect fines nevertheless we ostracize (nidoi) the assailant until they placate the victim and when they give the appropriate amount then we free them." Today when we don't ostracize (nidoi) the advisable approach is to put pressure on the assailant that he is to be ostracized in various ways as a substitute for nidoi. In the case where the assailant has signed an agreement which includes the right of the judge to decide what is best then it is also possible to obligate him to pay money.

Also a good suggestion is that where there is communication between the sides such as in the case of teachers (the majority of cases of abuse are these types) – one should insert an explicit clause in the agreement between the two sides which states that the abuser is obligated to pay according to the decision of the judge. It is also a good idea to specify that the plaintiff is the parent of the child and where that is not possible or if they don't want to - then the principal should be listed.

Rav Yehuda Silman[40](**Yeschurun 22**)**: Question:** I had previously received a query from America concerning the issue of informing the government authorities in a case of a teacher sexually abusing his student. The question was whether it is permitted or even a mitzva to be involved in reporting the matter to the secular authorities. I replied [Yeschurun 15 page 661] that there are number of different ways

Responsa & comments of Gedolim

to judge the matter. 1) **Viewing the abuser as a rodef** (pursuer) [I mentioned in the previous article that this does not apply in the case of a male above the age of 13 or a girl above the age of 12 when the adult does it with their consent.]. 2) **Stopping the abuser from sinning**. I brought the dispute between the Ketzos and the Nesivos HaMishpat…and the Yam Shel Shlomo and the Chasam Sofer. However it is agreed by all of these sources is that a person of distinguished status (chashiv) is able to stop another from committing a prohibited act. 3) **The position of Shulchan Aruch (C.M. 2)** that a beis din is able to flog and punish in order to protect society – in a manner which is not prescribed by the Torah. Therefore in a case like ours in which experience has shown that a sex abuser is able to ruin many people – everyone agrees that beis din can punish in ways not prescribed by the Torah.[In the earlier article I pointed out there are significant differences between these approaches. If you take the perspective of separating the abuser from sinning then if the teacher is fired then there is no longer a need to act since he has lost his primary opportunity to sin but of course it depends on the nature of the crime. In contrast if the concern is protecting society then the perpetrator should still be reported even if he has been fired.] 4) **The view expressed in Bava Metzia (83b)** concerning R' Eliezar bar Rav Shimon who was involved in capturing thieves because the king had commanded him to do so. I brought the dispute amongst the rishonim was to whether or not the halacha is in accord with R' Eliezar or not. In the original article I was inclined to the view that in the case of sexual abuse since the perpetrator is not executed but is imprisoned to protect society then perhaps all would agree that it is permitted to report him to the authorities.

Furthermore in the original article it was concluded that that it is obvious that there is no need to have witnesses that meet the standards required by the Torah but even less than that is sufficient and I cited a number of rishonim. The reason is reporting the teacher to the secular authorities is not punishment requiring a beis din but is an action mandated by secular law (in the Diaspora) or in order to separate the abuser from committing sin. In addition according to the reason that even in the case of a possible rodef it is permitted to inform the authorities – it is obvious that is permitted without proper witnesses since all that is required is that there be the possibility that he is an abuser.

Now you are asking a new question regarding which beis din is appropriate to judge these matters and what is the appropriate way to decide these cases. Some say

Child & Domestic Abuse

that it is necessary to convene a beis din in which both sides are present because otherwise it is impossible to establish the truth of the matter. But some say just the opposite and assert that it is not necessary to convene a beis din with both sides present and that in fact a beis din or even a rav is not needed at all. Rather what is needed is to involve the government authorities as soon as possible since only they have the legal right and actual ability to deal with these matters.... On the one hand concerning the legal requirement - it is clear that there is no need to convene a beis din in the presence of both sides since the basis of the permission to report the perpetrator to the secular authorities is either because he is a possible rodef (pursuer) or to separate him from sinning or because of the government mandates reporting. In fact these cases do not require a beis din and we need to merely consider the possible loss versus the possible gain. If the accusations are in fact true then we are dealing with a case of saving a person from being harmed. While if the accusations are in fact not true then in general then the government will free him. On the other hand it is certain that it is impossible that everyone can take responsibility for deciding whether to inform the secular authorities. That is because the majority of people do not have the prerequisite Torah knowledge or professional knowledge to establish whether the evidence is serious and the concern is genuine. Thus of necessity these matters should only be dealt with by an established beis din or at least an experience rabbi who has had a lot of experience dealing with cases of abuse. It is also clear that the beis din or the rav needs to make the decision only after appropriate consultation with professionals. R' Shabtei Sofer has written, "I know that a person who has a bit of knowledge but has not mastered it thinks that he know it all ..."

Rav Yitzchok Weiss –child abuse

Minchas Yitzchok[41]**(8:148):** Is it permitted to report to the police reckless drivers who are a danger to other motorists and pedestrians? Concerning the question regarding motorists who drive their vehicles in a manner which endangers all those who are on the road with them by means of the means different scenarios that are described in his letter. Is it permitted to report them to the police? This will typically result in a monetary punishment or the cancellation of their driver's license for a fixed period or incarceration in jail and it serves as a deterrent to actions which endanger others. Answer: Even though halacha prohibits causing a Jew to be given bodily or financially to the secular justice system, nevertheless a Jew who endangers other people is not included in this prohibition. This is explicitly stated by the Rambam

Responsa & comments of Gedolim

(Hilchos Chovel u'Mazik 8:11) and Shulchan Aruch (C.M. 388:12): "All those who disturb the community and cause it distress it is permitted to give them over to the secular government to be punished whether by beating, imprisonment or fines…" It is obvious that all those who drive carelessly and in a wild manner, endanger the lives of all those are near them. We in fact have been commanded to avoid danger and to prevent it from happening. Perhaps by taking actions against these drivers it will prevent danger and reduce the number of accidents. There is a difficulty however. The Rambam (Hilchos Chovel u'Mazik 8:9) states that it is prohibited to hand over a person to the secular government whether physically or financially even if he is wicked and even if he disturbs and distresses… And then the Rambam (Hilchos Chovel u'Mazik 8:11) states, "And thus all those who disturb and distress the society it is permitted to hand them over to the secular government to be beaten or imprisoned or fined.." What is the source of the distinction that the Rambam makes between those who disturb individuals and those who disturb the community? I could not find a source in the standard commentaries on the Rambam. However I found a source in the Chasam Sofer and his son the Ksav Sofer on their commentary to Gittin (7) and this supports the view of the Rivash (239). The Rivash notes, "If someone is disturbing and distressing the community then he should be punished according to what the beis din sees fit as we find in the Rambam (Hilchos Chovel u'Mazik 8:5): 'All those who disturb and distress the community it permitted to give them to the judges to be beaten, or jailed or to be fined - while if it only concerns an individual it is prohibited.' And similarly when the beis din sees a need to restore order to that generation…and the needs of the time require and they want to punish more than the halacha specifies for the sake of preserving society… they are permitted…" This ruling of the Rivash is cited by the Rema (C.M. 388:15). Thus we see from the Rivash- based on the explanation of the Rambam by the Chasam Sofer and the Ksav Sofer - that for an individual who is only being verbally abused it prohibited to report his abuser to the secular authorities. But that verbal abuse of the community is sufficient justification to call the police or surely to have him punished by a Jewish court…. However the Sema (C.M. 388:30):"This that the abuser is not reported to the secular authorities is only when he is verbally abusive but if he causes financial loss and surely if he beats him or causes bodily suffering it is permitted to report him to the secular authorities as is stated in the Rema and the Darchei Moshe. See also the Tur (C.M. 425:2)." This distinction is readily seen according to the Chasam Sofer's explanation of the Rambam… Rashi also would seem to support the idea that if the

Child & Domestic Abuse

abuser caused a loss of money and forgery then it is permitted to report him… The Rambam (Chovel u'Mazik 8:11) seems to being saying that only when it is verbal abuse that the abuser is not reported to the police but if he causes actually loss than it is permitted to prevent him suffering a loss. This is also the Rema (C.M. 388:9) and the Shach (C.M. 388:59-60)…The reason that the moser can be reported to the police is because he has the status of a rodef (pursuer) - as we find stated in the Rema (C.M. 388:12) and in the Sema (C.M. 388:29). The law of rodef is discussed in Shulchan Aruch (C.M. 425:1). Every Jew has the obligation to save others from a rodef according to the procedure discussed there. The Rema (C.M. 388:12) states that the rodef is someone who endangers the community such as a counterfeiter and it is permitted to report him to the police after warning him to stop…. Returning to our question, it is obvious that someone who drives at excessive speeds and thus cannot stop quickly enough when needed without causing an accident - has the status of a rodef (pursuer) even if his behavior was much less serious. … If after warning him he continues to act in this way, it is permitted to report him to the police. It is obvious that this is true for the other behaviors mentioned such as stopping at stop signs which enable pedestrians to cross the street or if he is dangerously tailgating the car in front of him. The same applies if he is driving without a license – all of these are in the category of rodef which endangers himself and others. Even if he doesn't intend to endanger others he is still considered a rodef. Also included is if he stops his car in a way that endangers pedestrians or by parking on the sidewalk which forces the pedestrians to go into the street or any of the other ways that that are described in the letter. All of these are equivalent to digging a pit in the public area… However as is explicit in Shulchan Aruch in all these laws – whether it is rodef (Shulchan Aruch C.M. 425) or moser (Shulchan Aruch 388:10) or whether it counterfeiting – before the perpetrator is reported to the police he needs to be formerly warned. Also in our case he should not be reported without beis din first warning him. Therefore those who are involved in this mitzva of life saving should first go to beis din and to present their claims before them…

Rav Yosef Shalom Eliashiv – child abuse

Rav Yosef Eliashiv[42]**(Nishmas Avraham 4:208-211):** Rav Eliashiv told me that there is in fact no difference in halacha between a teacher who is molesting boys or girls since in both cases we are talking about severe mental damages and danger to the public. He cited the Beis Yosef who cites the Rashba regarding R' Eliezar ben Rav

Responsa & comments of Gedolim

Shimon (Bava Metzia 83a) who reported thieves to the government… Regarding this Rav Eliashiv said that we learn from this that surely in the case of child abuse which is more severe then theft that it would be permitted to first report it to the principal of the school and if he doesn't do anything to report the matter to the police even in the Diaspora.

Rav Yosef Eliashiv[43]**(Nishmas Avraham 4:208-211): Rav Eliashiv** told me that it is permitted for a doctor to report the life threatening abuse to the authorities even when there is a possibility [in the Diaspora] that the child will be sent to a non-Jewish family or institution. However the doctor is then required to the best of his ability to see that the child is transferred to a Jewish family or institution.

Rav Yosef Eliashiv[44]**(Nishmas Avraham 4:208-211):** A child or baby is brought to the hospital with signs of "battered child" syndrome i.e., with many fractures in his skull or body or internal bleeding because of blows or hard kicks or with severe burns either from electric or boiling water and the like that were done cruelly and intentionally by one or both of his parents. It is prohibited after the completion of treatment to return him to his house because then beatings would just continue until he died. Because of the real danger to his life, the doctor is obligated to notify the courts and then by means of a court order, the child will be transferred to a foster family or institution. It would seem that there is no prohibition of moser (informing) since we are dealing with a life-threatening situation and the parents have the halachic status of rodef (pursuer). Therefore it is permitted to inform the authorities even if the child will automatically be removed from the parents and given to a family or institution which is not religious. However it is obvious that the beis din has to do whatever is in its power to try and ensure that the child is transferred to a family or institution which is observant And particularly in the Diaspora, the beis din has to be concerned that the child not be transferred to a non-Jewish family or institution. …

Rav Yosef Eliashiv[45]**(Kovetz Teshuvos 3:231):** … **Question:** If someone is sexually abusing a boy a girl in circumstances which we can't stop him from continuing his evil deeds – is it permissible to notify the government authorities? **Answer:** Rashba (3:393) states: "My view is that if the witnesses are believed by the judges, then it is permitted to punish the accused financially or physically depending upon what the judges think is appropriate to be beneficial to society. Because if we insist on doing only what is specified by Torah law and not to punish except as

Child & Domestic Abuse

specified in the Torah – the world will end up destroyed. That is because the elementary rules of a functioning society will be breached and consequently it will be ruined. It is an established practice to punish those who physically harm others…Every community makes judgments in order to preserve it and this is true in every generation and every place according to what is perceived as the needs of the times. For example we see (Sanhedrin 58b) that Rav Huna, who was in Babylonia, would amputate hands as punishment. Therefore these judges you referred to who punished the accused not in accord with Torah law – if they saw the need for it to preserve the society – they have correctly acted according to the halacha. This is true when there is a specific order from the king as we see in the case of R' Eliezar the son of R' Shimon bar Yochai in Bava Metzia (83a)." We learn from the Rashba's words that when action is needed for the well being of society (tikun olam), that the Jewish sages have the ability in every generation to act to preserve the society and to repair breaches – even when there isn't a specific order from the king. The Ritva (Bava Metzia 83b) has stated that this order of the king is "if the king says to capture certain criminals, even though the government will judge without witnesses and warning [as required by Torah law] and there is no functioning Sanhedrin [as required by Torah law] – it is still permitted since he is acting as the agent of the king. Since it is the law of the land to execute criminals without the testimony of witnesses and warning - as it states [Shmuel 2' 1:5-16] that Dovid killed the Amalekite ger who had acceded to Shaul's request to kill him -the agent of the king is like him." However according to what has been said, in a matter which is needed for the well being of society (tikun olam), it is not needed to have been ordered to act by the king [in order to act as needed]. However, it is permitted to notify the government authorities only in the case which it is certain that the accused has been sexually abusing children. Informing the authorities in such a case is clearly something for the well being of the society (tikun olam). However in a case where there is no proof that this activity is happening but it is merely a conjecture or suspicion, if we permit the calling of the authorities - not only would it not be an improvement (tikun olam) - but it would destroy society. That is because it is possible that allegations are being made solely because of some bitterness the student has against his teacher or because of some unfounded fantasy. As a result of these false allegations the accused will be placed in a situation for which death is better than life – even though he is innocent. Therefore I do not see any justification for calling the authorities in such circumstances.

Responsa & comments of Gedolim

Rav Yosef Eliashiv[46]**(Divrei Sinai page 45-46): Question:** On a number of occasions money has been stolen from the local religious affairs office. It appears that the thief is one of the employees. However we don't have the means of bringing about a confession. The question is whether it is permitted to turn to the police who after investigation - if they are successful in getting a confession - will bring the person to judgment in a secular court. The consequences of this would be very serious since we suspect someone who has a large family and in addition since he is someone who is involved in religious work it will result in chilul hashem (desecration of G-d's name), Heaven forbid! On the other hand, public money is missing and who knows what else. **Answer:** See Panim Me'eros (2:155) concerning our issue in which someone found an open chest from which much was stolen. There is reasonable circumstantial evidence that one of the workers was the thief. He was asked whether it was permissible to inform the secular authorities and that this will lead to him to confess … However at the end the Panim Me'eros concludes, "It is improper to turn a Jew over to secular authorities as our Sages say they will treat him like a trapped animal and there is concern that if he confesses they will kill him." From here it is clear that this ruling is not applicable in our times. Therefore it is permitted to turn to the police. However since you raise the concern that this will lead to a chilul hashem, I can't render an opinion concerning this since I don't know how to evaluate it and therefore the matter must be determined by your evaluation.

Rav Yosef Eliashiv[47]**(Yeschurun 15:642): Question:** In a case where the parents are abusing the children physically the secular law requires that the matter be reported to the police and the secular government might take the children from the parents custody to place them with another family – possibly even a non-Jewish family until they can investigate the matter – is it permitted to report the matter to the police when it is known that the child is in fact being abuse? **Answer:** The answer to the question is dependent on a number of factors. If the child's parents are observant of Torah and mitzvos and they have raised the child to be observant then to given the child to a non-Jews family or even a secular Jewish family is giving the child over to idolatry. That is because there is no doubt that this will damage the soul of the child even if it is for a short period of time and this will have harmful consequences also on his future upbringing. [We are only talking about a case of abuse which is not life threatening]. We also have to evaluate what is meant by abuse since the secular perspective is entirely different than ours. Because of the complexity of the issue

Child & Domestic Abuse

every case needs to be evaluated carefully by a talmid chachom who is great in scholarship and fear of heaven.

Rav Yitzchok Silberstein (Zohar #11 2003 pps 221-222): Removing an abused girl from her mother's custody. Question: A nine-year-old girl is being severely beaten and her mother is suspected. Her mother is a widow who has psychological problems who sometimes gives her daughter sleeping pills because she works until midnight cleaning houses. There are also days where she doesn't give her hot meals…. The question is whether to take the daughter from her mother's custody and to put her in a foster home to improve the daughters life in that she will eat properly and have a warm and secure family and she will learn what normal behavior is – or perhaps not since the mother has threatened suicide if her daughter is taken away… It is important to note that the mother is opposed to all alternatives such as a boarding school or receiving help of any type and she threatens suicide. **Answer:** This is a very difficult question and I asked one of the gedolim who replied, That it was very difficult to avoid the tears of the mother and her threat to commit suicide. He said that it was beyond our ability to properly evaluate and weigh these issues. Thus we can do nothing."

Let me clarify this psak. On the one hand, the daughter is not actually in mortal danger that we need to be worried that perhaps she will die from lack of food or from the beatings or difficult work. It also seems that the mother is not forcing her to swallow life-threatening pills. On the other hand, the mother has threatened to commit suicide if her daughter is taken from her. While it is true that people sometimes make threats that they don't carry out (Shavuos 46), but the Chofetz Chaim (Be'er Mayim Chaim Rechilus 9:12) has ruled that concerning life and death issues we need to be concerned about threats. This is seen from the incident with Gedaliya who was told someone threatened to kill him. When it comes to life and death, we need to take seriously even an unlikely danger. Furthermore in our case the doctors have agreed that it is possible that the mother will commit suicide…. In this case where we want to remove her daughter from her custody when the daughter's life is not actually being threatened – who says that the daughter's life is more important than the mother's? Perhaps the life of the mother is more in endangered than that of the daughter? This my explanation of the gadol's ruling of not removing the daughter from the mother's custody.

Responsa & comments of Gedolim

I presented the facts before Rav Eliashiv and he said the following. "Do not take the child from the custody of the mother who threatens to commit suicide – based entirely on circumstantial evidence of beatings that seem to done by the mother. As long as there are not actual witnesses that testify before us that they saw the mother cruelly beating her – it is impossible to remove the daughter from her custody. That is because it is a case of pikuach nefesh also for the mother – in particular since the daughter has not requested to be removed from her mother's custody. Similarly it is impossible to remove money from another person based on circumstantial evidence as is explained in Bava Basra (93a)… It would be different if the circumstantial evidence is absolutely clear that the mother is beating her such as if we find that the daughter has bite marks on her back which obviously can not be self-inflicted. The fact that the mother gives her daughter sleeping pills is also not a reason to take the daughter from her custody – since it is not clear that it is dangerous. Therefore we must do everything possible through the neighbors and friends who can speak persuasively with the mother or threaten her. But it is difficult to remove the daughter from the mother.

However if witnesses comes and testify before us that the mother is viciously beating her daughter then we are obligated to remove her from her mother's custody. This is so even though there is a small possibility that she might commit suicide. That is because it is not the daughter's fault so why should she have her life endangered because of the concern that her mother might commit suicide. Therefore when there are witnesses the daughter should be removed from her mother's custody."

Summary: 1) If it is clear that the mother is viciously beating her daughter, the daughter should be removed from her custody and we are not concerned with the mother's threat to commit suicide. 2) If no one has actually witnessed the mother beating her daughter but we deduce it from circumstantial evidence – there is no basis of removing the daughter from the mother. That is because the mother's life is also possibly endangered. Thus we are forced to do nothing (shev v'al taaseh). All we can do is make efforts through talking and deeds to try to stop the mother from beating her daughter. Heaven should be merciful.

Shulchan Aruch – self defense

Shulchan Aruch[48](**C. M. 2:1**): Every court – even those that do not have semicha from Israel – if they see that the see that the people is corrupted by sin (and thus it is

Child & Domestic Abuse

an emergency situation) can issue judgments whether concerning capital punishment or financial matters or any other punishments even without testimony according to Torah standards. If the transgressor is a powerful person than it is possible to punish him through the agency of non-Jews. Furthermore the court has the power to appropriate his money and to do with it what they see fit to strengthen the community. All the activities of the court need to be for the sake of heaven. This license to go beyond the letter of the law is specifically only for the greatest rabbis of the generation or the community leaders. It has been the practice in every place that the community leaders have the status similar to that of the Sanhedrin in that they can give beatings and punishments as well as appropriate a person's property – all according to the local practice. Even though there are those poskim which disagree and say that the local communities authorities do not have such powers but can only pressure the community according to the local practices or their actions need to be agreed upon by everyone. However according to these poskim they have no power to make any changes in law in situations where there is benefit to one party and loss to another or to appropriate someone's money without his agreement. Nevertheless one should follow the practices of the city. And surely these powers exist in fact everyone member of the community accepts that the leaders have these powers. The achronim mention in their responsa that some who is deserving of lashes should give 40 gold coins as a substitute for the 40 lashes. This is not according to the letter of the law but is only an emergency measure. Therefore the court has the emergency power to administer lashes or to take money according to what they see are the needs of the times (migder milsa).

Shulchan Aruch[49]**(C.M. 4:1):** A person can act on his rights without receiving a ruling from beis din. For example if he sees one of his possessions in the hands of someone who stole it from him, he is able to take it from that person. If the thief resists he has the right to beat him until he lets him have the object back – if he can not get it back any other way. This right exists even if there is no loss if he waits to go to beis din first. However this right of action is only valid if he is able to clearly ascertain that the object is his so that he is taking it according to the law. However he has no right to take an object just because the person owes him money...

Shulchan Aruch[50]**(C.M. 26:2):** If the non-Jews are the controlling power and the litigant is powerful in his own right and therefore the person can not recover what is his by the authority of the Jewish court – he should first summon his opponent to the

Responsa & comments of Gedolim

Jewish court. If his opponent refuses to go – he should obtain permission from the Jewish court and then use the non-Jewish court to recover what is his from his opponent. **Rema:** The Jewish court has the right to go to the non-Jewish court and to testify that one person owes the other money. All this is only if one of the litigants refuses to obey the Jewish court. Otherwise it is prohibited for a Jewish court to give authorization for Jews to have their dispute presented to a non-Jewish court..

Shulchan Aruch[51](**C.M. 35:14**): A woman is not a valid witness…**Rema:** All those who are invalid witnesses are invalid even in circumstances where Jewish men are usually not found. However all this is according to the strict letter of the law, but there are those who say that there is an ancient decree regarding a place where men are not normally found such as the women's section of a synagogue or any other circumstances where only women are typically present and not men. This decree also applies in regards to facts that women pay attention to and men don't - such as to testify that "this woman wore these clothes." In these cases a woman's testimony is believed (Terumas HaDeshen 353 and Aguda asara yuchsin). Therefore there are those who say that even one woman or a relative or child is believed concerning physical abuse or the shaming of a talmid chachom or other disputes and informing. That is simple because it is not normal to invite valid witnesses nor is there time to summon them to these events (Maharik 179, Maharam M'Rizborg, Kol Bo #116). However these alternative witnesses are only believed when they claim that they are certain of what they are saying (Maharik 93).

Shulchan Aruch[52](**C.M. 388:12**): Whoever is a informant (moser) regarding the community and harasses it – it is permitted to hand over that individual to the non-Jewish government to be beaten, imprisoned or to be fined. However if this individual only harasses an individual it is prohibited to hand him over to the secular government.

Shulchan Aruch[53](**C.M. 388:9**): It is prohibited to inform on a Jew – either concerning himself or his money - to non-Jews who are in power by force. This is prohibited even if he is a wicked person and a sinner and even if he causes aggravation and trouble to the potential informer. **Rema:** But the prohibition is only if he aggravates him with words. However if the Jew informs on him then it is permitted to inform on the Jew who informed. Because he has the right to kill the one who informed on him because of the fear the informer will reciprocate and inform on him

Child & Domestic Abuse

to the secular authorities (Rosh 17:1, Rashba #181) or if it is impossible to save himself another way. However if he can he should save himself another way. Thus it is like two people who inform on each other. Whoever causes the greatest loss is obligated to pay the difference. Whoever gives over a Jew into the hands of non-Jews – whether physically or monetarily – he has no portion in the world to come.

Shulchan Aruch[54](**C.M. 421:13**): Similarly when someone sees another Jew hitting someone and he is not able to stop the assailant without hitting him – he is able to hit the assailant in order to stop him from sinning. **Rema:** And this is also the case with anyone in your control. If you see him sinning – it is allowed to hit and punish him in order to stop him from sinning **and it is not necessary to bring him to beis din.**

Tzitz Eliezar – child abuse

Tzitz Eliezar[55](**Nishmas Avraham 4:208-211**): Rav Waldenburg wrote to me that if there are well founded fears that that the parents will likely start hitting him again and perhaps even more severely until he dies – then in such a case where the doctor only informs the police about the situation of the child and asks that they investigate to save the child from his parents – then he is obligated to do this in order to save the live of a Jew from death. What the police do afterwards in order to save the child the doctor is only one indirect causal force and thus it is not actually considered lifnei ivair because it is not 100% certain that the child will be transferred to a non-Jewish institution or to one that is not religious. In addition the child until he becomes an adult does not commit any sin and when he grows up he will it is possible that they will return him to a place where he will be able to observe a Jewish life.

Tzitz Eliezer[56](**Nishmas Avraham 4:208-211**): If we are discussing a case of incest, for example the father is raping his little daughter repeatedly then the father has the status of rodef as in the case of life threatening physical abuse... There is no difference between the status of rodef for causing physical danger and for rape. The father committing incest is punishable by kares even though she is only a child. Therefore we have an obligation to free him from this sin...

Tzitz Eliezer[57](**Nishmas Avraham 4:208-211**): If we are talking about little children being raped in a school by a teacher, in the case of boys it is a sin punishable by execution by beis din and therefore it is the perpetrators has the status of rodef. This means he can be reported to the authorities. However if these disgusting acts are

Responsa & comments of Gedolim

committed with girls, then it would be permitted for the doctor to reveal the matter to the principal. If the principal doesn't do anything then it would be permitted to report the matter to the police even in the Diaspora. That is because this is harm being done to the many therefore there is no prohibition of mesira [C.M. 388:12 according to Shach and Gra]. In fact not only is it permitted but he is obligated to report the teacher so that he does not continue these bad acts not only in this school but in any other school. However it is clear that in all cases the doctor can not take any steps unless he is first convinced that he has his facts right and that he consults with a major rabbi because this is a matter of life and death. … The Tzitz Eliezer wrote to me that in the case of sexual molesting done by a teacher that there is an additional reason that it is permitted to report him to the police. The since Shulchan Aruch (C.M. 388:12) permits reporting a person who distresses and harms the public then surely in the case of child abuse it would be permitted.

Tzitz Eliezer[58]**(Nishmas Avraham 4:208-211):** A child or baby is brought to the hospital with signs of "battered child" syndrome i.e., with many fractures in his skull or body or internal bleeding because of blows or hard kicks or with severe burns either from electric or boiling water and the like that were done cruelly and intentionally by one or both of his parents. It is prohibited after the completion of treatment to return him to his house because then beatings would just continue until he died. Because of the real danger to his life, the doctor is obligated to notify the courts and then by means of a court order, the child will be transferred to a foster family or institution. It would seem that there is no prohibition of moser (informing) since we are dealing with a life-threatening situation and the parents have the halachic status of rodef (pursuer). Therefore it is permitted to inform the authorities even if the child will automatically be removed from the parents and given to a family or institution which is not religious. However it is obvious that the beis din has to do whatever is in its power to try and ensure that the child is transferred to a family or institution which is observant And particularly in the Diaspora, the beis din has to be concerned that the child not be transferred to a non-Jewish family or institution. … Rav Waldenburg (Tzitz Eliezer 19:52) wrote to me that if there are well founded fears that that the parents will likely start hitting him again and perhaps even more severely until he dies – then in such a case where the doctor only informs the police about the situation of the child and asks that they investigate to save the child from his parents – then he is obligated to do this in order to save the live of a Jew from death. What the police do

Child & Domestic Abuse

afterwards in order to save the child the doctor is only one indirect causal force and thus it is not actually considered lifnei ivair because it is not 100% certain that the child will be transferred to a non-Jewish institution or to one that is not religious. In addition the child until he becomes an adult does not commit any sin and when he grows up he will it is possible that they will return him to a place where he will be able to observe a Jewish life.

Tztiz Eliezer[59](15:13.1): **Question**: A doctor discovered that his patient has defective vision which can cause him to have auto accidents when driving under certain circumstances – such as under the conditions of his job or at night…. The patient doesn't want to stop driving or to change his job. Is the doctor obligated to keep this confidential or is he obligated to notify the appropriate agency (whether governmental or his employer) concerning this matter? It is likely that this information will cause his patient economic damage or his interaction with society. What if the patient asks him to keep this confidential and he promises to stop from driving under the dangerous circumstances – but the doctor is not convinced that he can be believed to stop driving? **Answer**: There is no question that the doctor is obligated to notify the appropriate governmental agency or employer so that they can have the patient drive within his limitation. Even if the patient requests the doctor to keep his illness a secret and promises to stop driving… As long as the doctor is not convinced that he will do so – he is obligated to notify the agencies. It is also obvious that if the doctor is summoned to testify concerning this that he must go and testify. [Furthermore his oath as a doctor to keep medical information secret does not apply to these cases nor does a private oath to the patient. That is because it would mean that he is taking an oath to nullify a mitzva and thus it is simply invalid. His oath as a doctor shouldn't apply to information which if it is withheld would constitute a crime. (All this is discussed in greater detail in Tztiz Eliezer 3:81 part 2 and 3.)]. But even if he was not summoned he is still obligated to take the initiative to inform the appropriate agencies because otherwise the patient might be a danger to the lives of others. If the doctor refrains from notifying the agencies than he has transgressed the Torah command of "not standing by the blood of your fellow." Therefore the doctor should not take into consideration that his act of informing might cause economic or social damage. That is because nothing stands in the way of saving life (pikuach nefesh). I want to add to this what I found in the Pischei Teshuva (O.C. 156): "And I want to comment on the issue that all the mussar books make a big deal about

Responsa & comments of Gedolim

speaking lashon harah, but I want to make a big deal about the opposite. That is the greater and more common sin of refraining from speaking lashon harah when it is needed to save a person from harm ..." These words express much clearer and forcefully what I have been saying. The Pischei Teshuva notes that a person's intent should not be to harm the person he is speaking about but rather for the benefit of the person he is telling and others that he is saving from harm. Because by focusing on helping he fulfills a great inestimable mitzva. I also found a similar case in the Chelkas Yaakov (3:136) concerning a young man who the doctor found had cancer. The young man and his family didn't know about it at all. The man was engaged to marry a young woman. His question was whether the doctor was obligated to reveal the sickness to his fiancée as well as well as the fact that he only had at most one or two years to live. It was obvious that if she found out this information she would not marry him. The Chelkas Yaakov replied that the doctor was obligated to inform the fiancée because the main halacha issue is that the doctor should not violate the mitzva of "not standing by the blood of your fellow." He based his psak on the Rambam (Hilchos Rotzeach 1:14) and Shulchan Aruch (C.M. 426).... So surely this is true in our case where the matter might cause actual danger to the lives of others. So there is absolutely no question that if the doctor does not reveal the information to the appropriate agencies now, he will be transgressing by this withholding - of the prohibition of "not standing by the blood of your fellow." Therefore it is absolutely permitted for the doctor and also is clearly obligatory for him to notify the appropriate government agency or employer concerning the limitation of his patients vision.

Tzitz Eliezer[60]**(19:52): Question 1 – Physically abused child -** Unfortunately it is not rare that a child is brought to the hospital covered by bruises and fractures and concussions as well as damage to internal organs - as the result of being beaten or with severe burns which are the result of boiling water or cigarettes. These injuries are severe enough to be life threatening (pikuach nefesh). These wounds were made deliberately by one or both of the child's parents – as I have written in my sefer Tzitz Eliezer (C.M. 424:2 page 219). When a complaint is filed with the police, then after the treatment is complete and the child is released from the hospital – he is transferred by means of an order from the secular court to a foster family or institution in order to save him from his parents. That is because there have been no small number of cases where the child was return to his home and he was beaten to death afterwards. My question is what is the halacha for a doctor who knows that there is a good chance that

Child & Domestic Abuse

the child will be transferred to a home or institution which is not religious or even outside of Israel to a home or institution of non-Jews. Should he still file a complaint with the police or not? **Question 2 – In a case where the father repeated rapes his young daughter and there is no danger to her life** – what are the answers to the questions raised in the previous case? **Question 3 – It would seem that it would be permitted to inform the police (C.M. 388:12)** according to the text of the Shach and Gra and this is also true **for the case of the beaten child which is dealing with pikuach nefesh and therefore the parents have the status of rodef. However what is the halacha in the second case which deals with incestual rape? This seems to be a different problem because it states in Shulchan Aruch (388:9) that "it is prohibited to inform on him even if he is a wicked person and even if he causes the person distress and suffering"?** Is the Shulchan Aruch referring to a situation such as the incestual rape of a young daughter where there is clearly damage both physically as psychologically? Furthermore it is clear to me that every single case requires the doctor - prior to calling the police - to consult with an established expert posek who will carefully weigh the facts in each case to establish its true nature. However I strongly desire to hear the Rav's views in these painful cases. **Answer – Concerning the first case of the physically abused child** – In my humble opinion it would appear that **if there is a clearly established basis that the child's parents are almost certainly going to continue viciously beat him when he returns home** and that it is possible that they might kill him, in such circumstances since the doctor is only informing the police of the facts together with a request to save the child from the parents – then the doctor is obligated to inform the police in order to save the life of a Jew from being destroyed. What the government agency does after he informs the police in order to save the child – the doctor has served only as an indirect cause. Therefore the doctor doesn't have to worry that he has actually violated the prohibition of lifnei ivair (putting a stumbling block before the blind) – since it is not 100% certain that they will transfer the child from his home to a non-Jewish institution or one that is not observant of the Jewish religion. [See Avoda Zara 15 as well as Tevuas Shor (15:24) who learns from this gemora that the prohibition of lifnei ivair only applies when there is definitely a stumbling block and this is also the view of other poskim]. Furthermore the child is not sinning by being placed in a non-Jewish environment until he grows up. When he grows up is it reasonable that the will return to an environment where he is able to fully observe his religion. [See Chasam Sofer O.C. (#83) and Kaf HaChaim O.C. (#343:22)]. **However in a case of physical abuse**

Responsa & comments of Gedolim

where it can not be solidly established that it is actually pikuach nefesh (life threatening) then the case is merely one of determining what is in the best interest of the child. In such a non-life threatening case, it is prohibited to file a complaint with the police when it is highly likely that the child will be taken from his religious home or traditional home and be transferred to a non-Jewish institution or a non-observant Jewish one or one that is not even traditional. The exception being if his home is no different in religious observance than the institute to which they will likely transfer him. This governing principle is found in the Sifre (Ki Satze) where it states that those who cause others to sin are worse than if they had killed them. That is because the killer [only] takes the victim from this world but not the next. In contrast the one who causes sin causes him to lose both this world and the next. We find something similar in the Chochmas Adam (59:12): Do not give a child to a non-Jew for either schooling or to learn a trade – even when there is no concern for the physical life of the child such as when the teaching is done in a public place. Nevertheless is prohibited because the child might be attracted to the non-Jewish religion. It would appear to me that this rule can be generalized to prohibit giving the child to heretics - which are much worse than non-Jews - because Jewish heresy is more enticing." This can readily be generalized to our case. 2) **Concerning the second case where the father is repeatedly raping his little daughter and there is no concern that he will kill her – what is the halacha regarding the previous questions?** In my opinion the halacha is the same as it was in the first case where there was a concern for pikuach nefesh (life threatening). That is because the father has the status of rodef (pursuer) after prohibited sexual relations, which are, treated the same as one who is a rodef to kill someone. That is true only since the incestuous rape of his daughter entails the punishment of kares – even though she is just a child but that is the father's punishment and therefore there is a clear obligation to stop him… All this is in addition to the halachic fact that there is an obligation to save the girl from physical and psychological damage. Thus taking this all together the answer concerning calling the police is the same as in the case of physical abuse. Concerning the cases mentioned there were an additional two questions that were mentioned concerning the law of moser. In regards to the first case concerning physical danger, the parents have the status of rodef and therefore it is permitted to inform the police about them. However concerning the second case we have an apparent restriction imposed by the Shulchan Aruch (C.M. 388:9) which prohibits informing on a person who is a wicked person and sinner – even if he distresses and causes pain. Does the Shulchan Aruch

Child & Domestic Abuse

prohibit informing in the case where there is incestuous rape which includes physical and psychological damage? My reply is that first of all that just as in the first case of physical abuse if it is clear to him that there is a danger it is permitted to inform on him since the parents have the status of rodef. Similarly it is also permitted in the case of incestuous rape because the father is also a rodef – though after prohibited sexual relations rather than danger to life as I mentioned before. Secondly even if the sexual relationship with the child is not one that incurs the punishment of kares [and thus the rapist would not be considered a rodef] it is still permitted to inform the police. This is so both in order to save her from being raped and also in order to save the rapist from this wickedness. This that you have cited the Shulchan Aruch (C.M. 388:9) - which seems to prohibit informing the police even if he is a wicked person – that is not identical to our case. The Shulchan Aruch is not addressing the issue of informing on the wicked person in order to save him from his own actions but rather to inform on him for a different motivation. It is a case where they want to treat the wicked person in a degrading manner because he is a wicked person – in such a case it is prohibited by the Shulchan Aruch. In contrast in our case the motivation is to stop him from committing a sin by informing on him. With such a motivation it is permitted to inform on him. Furthermore it is permitted to inform on him to stop him from harming the young child. In addition this case is not at all the same as the Shulchan Aruch prohibits informing to save from suffering and anguish. The Shulchan Aruch's prohibition doesn't apply in our case where there is physical and psychological damage. Look at the Shulchan Aruch (C.M. 388:7 where the Rema says that there is a view that if a person is beaten by another person he is able to go and complain to the non-Jewish authorities – even if it causes his assailant great harm. Furthermore the Shach (C.M. 388:45) makes a similar distinction. He says that it is permitted to inform on the assailant in order to prevent the assailant from continuing his beatings. Therefore concerning the present case – it is obviously much more severe than a mere beating. Consequently it is permitted to inform on the rapist – both because it is like the case of an assailant who hits and even more important – so that he is prevented from raping her anymore. It is important to remember that the beis din is considered the protecting father of little children. 4) From that which has been presented here it is self evident that even **in the third case dealing a teacher molesting his young students – that it is permitted to inform the police about him**. This is simply a logical extension of what we have said. Since the third case is someone who is causing significant distress to the masses it is similar to what is stated openly in

Responsa & comments of Gedolim

Shulchan Aruch (C.M. 388:12) - as the questioner himself has correctly noted. 5) After all, I think it is necessary to add two more points for the sake of clarity. a) The question of mesira only is relevant when complaining to a non-Jewish court – not a Jewish court. This point is emphasized in Shulchan Aruch (C.M. 388:9): It is prohibited to handover a Jew to non-Jews… It is only in reference to giving over a Jew's money that it says (Shulchan Aruch 388:2): That there is no differences whether the money is given over to a non-Jew or to a Jew." b) Even concerning the non-Jewish courts it would appear that there is a difference between uncivilized countries and enlightened ones as is stated in the Aruch HaShulchan (C.M. 388:7): All that is written in the Talmud and poskim regarding the prohibition of moser – is referring to distance lands where a person's life and money are not secure because of the bandits and lawless people – even though they have a government as we find in various countries such as those in Africa… as opposed to the European countries. It is obvious from the words of the Aruch HaShulchan that he truly meant this and not out of fear of the government… As I mentioned, the above was written for the general clarification of the prohibition of moser. Side point: In addition to what we have said that the essential prohibition of moser is to hand the case to a non-Jewish court, but if the times require it and it is done with the permission of the beis din – there is a basis to say it is permitted in a situation where it is not possible for the Jewish court to handle the case. We find an example of this in the Mabit (1:22) concerning the imprisonment of a heretic by the non-Jewish government and the condition of freedom was to leave the country and to divorce his wife….

Child & Domestic Abuse

Hebrew Sources

[1] **פחתי תשובה (אורח חיים סימן קנו)**: ...וראיתי להזכיר פה ע"ד אשר כל הספרי מוסר הרעישו העולם על עון לה"ר ואנכי מרעיש העולם להיפוך עון גדול מזה וגם הוא מצוי יותר והוא מניעת עצמו מלדבר במקום הנצרך להציל את העשוק מיד עושקו. דרך משל במי שראה באחד שהוא אורב על חבירו בערמה על הדרך במדבר להרגו או שראה חותר מחתרת בלילה בביתו או בחנותו היתכן שימנע מלהודיע לחבירו שיזהר ממנו משום איסור לשון הרע הלא עונו גדול מנשוא שעובר על לא תעמוד על דם רעיך. וכן בענין ממון הוא בכלל השבת אבידה. ועתה מה לי חותר מחתרת או שראוה משרתיו גונבים ממונו בסתר או שותף גונב דעתו בעסק או שחבירו מטעהו במקח וממכר או שלוה מעות והוא גברא דלאו פרענא הוא. וכן בעיני שידוך והוא יודע שהוא איש רע ובליעל ורע להתחתן עמו כולן בכלל השבת אבידת גופו וממונו. ועתה איה לנו הגדר והגבול לומר עד פה תדבר ולא יותר. והכלל בזה שהדבר מסור ללב אם כונתו לרעת לרעת האחד הוא לשון הרע אבל אם כונתו לטובת השני להצילו ולשמרו הוא מצוה רבה.

וזהו לדעתי עומק כונת הירושלמי שהביא המ"א דמותר לדבר לה"ר על בעלי המחלוקת. ולכאורה קשה ע"ז מהא דאמרינן מ"ק (דף טז) דיליף דבשליח ב"ד אין בו משום לשון הרע מדהגיד למשה העיני האנשים ההם תנקר וכו' ומאי ראיה הא עדת קרח ה"ה בעלי המחלוקת. והוא אשר דברתי דודאי גם על בעל מחלוקת אין לספר בחנם רק בדבר המחלוקת שהוא צופה רעת חבירו אז מותר לגלות גנותו להצלת חבירו ולפ"ז מוכח שפיר דמה שאמר למשה מה שאמרו עדת קרח הוא בלא תועלת וע"כ הוא רק משום דשליח ב"ד מותר שוב מצאתי כן בגליון הש"ס על הירושלמי. ועתה כמה פעמים אנו רואים תקלת חבירו הפרוסה לרגליהם מאדם רע וכובשים פנינו באמרינו מה לנו להכניס בדבר אשר אינו נוגע לנו ועי' בתשו' מקום שמואל (סי' צא) אהא דמתאמרי באפי מרא לית ביה משום ל"ב היינו דוקא במתכוין לשם תוכחה אבל לא לקנתור ע"ש. ובדברים כאלו וכי"ב כבר אמרו חז"ל בדבר המסור ללב נאמר ויראת מאלהיך.

[2] **נדה (סא.)**: תנא: הוא הבור שמילא ישמעאל בן נתניה חללים, דכתיב (ירמיהו מא:ט) והבור אשר השליך שם ישמעאל את כל פגרי אנשים אשר הכה ביד גדליה. וכי גדליה הרגן ! אלא מתוך שהיה לו לחוש לעצת יוחנן בן קרח ולא חש - מעלה עליו הכתוב כאילו הרגן. אמר רבא: האי לישנא בישא, אע"פ דלקבולי לא מבעי - מיחש ליה מבעי....

[3] **ביאור הגר"א (אבן העזר קנד:ט)**: ואם רגיל כו'. כמ"ש בפ' ד' מיתות [סנהדרין נח:] דר"ה קץ ידא וכ"ש באשתו כנ"ל:

[4] **אור זרוע (ח"ג פסקי בבא קמא סימן קסא)**: מיכן יש ללמוד שאסור לאדם להכות את אשתו וגם חייב בנזקיה אם הזיקה. ואם הוא רגיל תדיר להכותה ולהבזותה ברבים כופין אותו להוציאה...

[5] **בית יוסף (אבן העזר קנד:ג)**: (ב) מצאתי בתשובת רבינו שמחה המכה את אשתו מקובלני שיש יותר להחמיר מבמכה את חבירו דבחבירו אינו חייב בכבודו ואשתו חייב לכבדה יותר מגופו (יבמות סוף סב:) והעושה כן יש להחרימו ולנדותו ולהלקותו ולענשו בכל מיני רידוי ואף לקוץ ידו אם רגיל בכך (סנהדרין נח: ורש"י שם ד"ה קץ ידא) ואם היא רוצה לצאת

126

Responsa & comments of Gedolim

יוציא ויתן כתובה. ואח"כ כתב תטילו שלום ביניהם ואם לא יעמוד הבעל בקיום השלום שאם יוסיף להכותה ולבזותה אנו מסכימים להיות מנודה ויעשוהו ע"י גוים לתת גט או עשה מה שישראל אומרים לך (גיטין פח:) ...

[6] **רמב"ם (הלכות חובל ומזיק ד:טז)**: ...הבעל שחבל באשתו חייב לשלם לה מיד כל הנזק והצער וכל הבושת והכל שלה ואין לבעל בהן פירות, ואם רצתה ליתן הדמים לאחר נותנת, וכזה הורו הגאונים, והבעל מרפא אותה כדרך שמרפא כל חליה.

[7] **רמ"א (אבן העזר קנד:ג)**... הגה: וכן איש שרגיל לכעוס ולהוציא אשתו מביתו תמיד, כופין אותו להוציא, כי ע"י אינו זנה לפעמים ופורש ממנה בתשמיש יותר מעונתה והוי כמורד ממזונות ותשמיש (תשובת הרשב"א סימן תרצ"ג). ועיין לעיל סימן ע' וע"ז. איש המכה אשתו, עבירה היא בידו כמכה חבירו. ואם רגיל הוא בכך, יש ביד ב"ד ליסרו ולהחרימו ולהלקותו בכל מיני רידוי וכפייה, ולהשביעו שלא יעשה עוד, ואם אינו ציית לדברי הב"ד י"א שכופין אותו להוציא, ובלבד שמתרין בו תחלה פעם אחת או שתים כי אינו מדרך בני ישראל להכות נשותיהם, ומעשה עובד כוכבים הוא. וכל זה כשהוא מתחיל, אבל אם מקללתו בחנם או מזלזלת אביו ואמו, והוכיחה בדברים ואינה משגחת עליו, י"א דמותר להכותה, וי"א דאפילו אשה רעה אסור להכותה. והסברא ראשונה היא עיקר. ואם אינו ידוע מי הגורם, אין הבעל נאמן לומר שהיא המתחלת, שכל הנשים בחזקת כשרות, ומושיבים ביניהם אחרים לראות בשל מי הרעה הזאת, ואם היא מקללתו חנם, יוצאת בלא כתובה. ונראה לי דוקא ברגילה בכך, ואחר ההתראה, וכמו שנתבאר לעיל סימן קט"ו. ואם הלכה מביתו וללוותה ואכלה, אם יצאתה מכח שהכה אותה תמיד, חייב לשלם (כל דברי הגה זו תמצא במרדכי פרק נערה בשם מוהר"ם וב"י סימן פ"ח), וכמו שנתבאר לעיל סימן ע'.

[8] **עזרא (ז:כו)**: כל די לא להוא עבד דתא די אלהך ודתא די מלכא אספרנא דינה להוא מתעבד מנה הן למות הן לשרשו לשרשי הן לענש נכסין ולאסורין:

[9] **מנחת יצחק (ח:קמח)**: בענין אם מותר למסור לשלטונות את אלו המסכנים עוברי דרך ע"י אי זהירות בהנהגתם בכלי רכב.

הנני בזה ע"ד שאלתו היות ויש כמה כמה הנהגים בכלי רכב באופן המסכן את כל מי שנמצא לידם בדרכים, או בכלי רכב הסמוכים להם, ע"י כמה וכמה אופנים שחשבם במכתבו, האם מותר למסרם לשלטונות, אשר בדרך כלל מענישים אותם בקנסות כספיים, או בשלילת הרשיון - נהיגה לתקופה מסויימת או במאסרים, למען ישמעו וייראו וימנעו מדברים המסכנים את הציבור ואף דעפ"י הלכה אסור למסור גופו או ממונו של ישראל לערכאות, אבל מי שמסכן הציבור אינו בכלל זה, וכמבואר ברמב"ם (חובל ומזיק ח:יא) ושו"ע (חו"מ שפח:יב) שכל המיצר הציבור ומצערן מותר למסרו ביד עכו"ם להכותו ולאסרו ולקנסו וכו', ודבר ברור שכל אלו שנוהגים באי זהירות ובצורה מופקרת מכניסים לסכנת נפשות את כל מי שנמצא בסמוך להם, והלא נצטוינו להתרחק מהסכנה, וכל דבר המביאים לידי סכנה, ואולי ע"י נקיטת אמצעים ופעולות נגדם נרחיק את הסכנה ויתמעטו האסונות עכת"ד.

הנה ברמב"ם (ה"ט) איתא אסור למסור האדם ביד /עכו"ם/ בין בגופו בין בממונו ואפילו היה רשע ובעל עבירות, ואפילו הי' מיצר ומצערו וכו' ואח"כ (בהי"א) כתב, וכן כל המיצר הציבור לציבור ומצערן מותר למסרו ביד עכו"ם להכותו ולאסרו ולקנסו וכו' כנ"ל. והנה חפשתי בנושאי כלים להרמב"ם להראות המראה מקום להחילוק בין יחיד לציבור ולא מצאתי,...

Child & Domestic Abuse

ובנותי בספרים ומצאתי את שאהבה נפשי, באב ובנו שראו את החידוש, ה"ה הגאוני עולם החת"ס והכת"ס ז"ל (בספריהם על מס' גיטין), שהעירו שם (גיטין ז.) על הרמב"ם דבמצער לציבור, דנושאי כליו לא הראו מקום לדין זה כנ"ל, וכתב החת"ס משום דמשמע מסוגיין (גיטין ז.) שם, דאי לאו דהוה לי' הצלה ע"י השכם והערב הי' מותר למוסרו, וזה שייך ביחיד לעצמו, אבל בציבור קדירא דבי שותפי מי יערוב וישכם בעד כולם, ע"כ מותר למוסרו עיי"ש, ואחריו בא בנו הגאון הכת"ס בספרו (גיטין) שם, ומילא את דברי אביו הגאון ז"ל, וכתב וז"ל ואאמ"ו זצ"ל בחידושיו נתקשה מנ"ל להרמב"ם הא (דמצער לציבור מותר למוסרו) ונדחק, והנ"ל כשנדקדק בלשון קרא בעוד רשע לנגדי, תיבת בעוד קשה עוד יותר, ונ"ל דהתורה הראה לנו דלא בזה שם לפי מחסום רק כ"ז שלא הרשיע רק נגדו, אבל כשציער לרבים, וכך דרכם של רשעים וכו' מראה אל ראה יצאו להרע ולצער רבים לא החשתי עוד וכו' עכ"ד. והרי שניהם נתכוונו לדבר אחד שמצאו מקור לדברי הרמב"ם הנ"ל בדברי הש"ס גיטין (ז.), ובזה יהי' רוי' לדברי הריב"ש כדלהלן. דהנה ראיתי בתשו' הריב"ש (סי' רל"ט) שכתב באמצע התשובה, וז"ל גם מה שאמר נגד המוקדמין אין ראוי להקרא מסירה וכו' אבל מכל מקום בהמשך מן הדברים הם נזק להקהל והוצאות ולבא במשפט עם זקני עמו ושריו, לא ימלט שמעון מהיות מיצר ומצער הצבור באמרו הדברים ההם, וראוי להענש על זה כפי מה שיראה בעיני הב"י כמ"ש הרמב"ם (חובל ומזיק ח:ה), וכן כל המיצר לצבור ומצער אותם מותר למוסרו ביד השופטים להכותם ולקנסו אבל מפני צער יחיד אסור למוסרו ע"כ. וכן אם יראה בעיני הב"ד שהדור פרוץ וכו' ולפי צורך ירצו להעניש יותר מן הדין משום מגדר מילתא וכו' הרשות בידם וכו' עכ"ל. ....., והנה דינו של הריב"ש הנ"ל, הביא ג"כ הרמ"א (חו"מ שפח:טו), ...ודאתאן מן דברי הריב"ש דאף בדברים בעלמא של חירוף וגידוף שייך הא דהרמב"ם לציבור וכו', דכל המצער לציבור וכו', והרי כל זה אתי שפיר מאד לפי"ד החת"ס והכת"ס דמקור מקומו טהור של דברי הרמב"ם הנ"ל, בדברי הש"ס דגיטין (ז.), דפיהרש"י העומדים עלי לחרף ולגדף, דש"מ תרתי, א' דביחיד משום צער של דברים אסור למוסרו, ב' דמשום צער הציבור מותר למוסרו אף לעכו"ם אף רק משום חירוף וגידוף כנ"ל, וא"כ מכ"ש לעונשו ע"י ישראל כדברי הריב"ש. ...., דהנה בסמ"ע שם (שפח:ל) כתב על דצער יחיד, וז"ל והיינו דוקא מפני צער דעלמא, אבל מסרו בממון, וכש"כ אם יסרו במכות ועונש הגוף מותר כמ"ש בס"א בהגה ועד"מ ס"ט וע"י בטור (תכה:סב) עכ"ל, והנה כ"ז ש"מ ג"כ מהא דגיטין שם, כמ"ש בחת"ס שם, דאע"ג דממה שפיהרש"י שם העומדים עלי לחרף ולגדף, י"ל משום שהאמת כך הי' בגניבא, אבל מהא שפיהרש"י שם, אקרא בעוד רשע לנגדי, מריבני ומקניטני, מוכח דפשיטא לרש"י דאם הי' מצערו בממון וזיוף מותר למוסרו, ואינו צריך להשכים ולהעריב כי הבא להורגך השכם להורגו, וכ"פ הרמב"ם (מחובל ומזיק ח:יא) וכו', אבל מפני צער יחיד אסור למוסרו וכו', משמע מצער בעלמא, אבל מפסידו מותר למוסרו שלא יפסידנו כמ"ש הרמ"א (חו"מ שפח:ט) וכו', ורש"י שם (שפח:נט וס') ....עכ"ל. ...והנה הטעם דהמוסר הוא משום שיש לו דין רודף כמ"ש ברמ"א (חו"מ שפח:יב) ובסמ"ע שם (חו"מ שפח:כט) עיי"ש, ודין רודף מבואר שם בש"ע /חו"מ/ (סי' תכ"ה ס"א), דכל ישראל מצווין להצילו, כפי סדר ההצלה המבואר שם, וכתב שם הרמ"א דמי שמסכן רבים כגון שעוסק בזיופים דינו כרודף ומותר למוסרו למלכות, וכ"כ שם /חו"מ/ (סי' שפח:יב), דמי שעוסק בזיופים ויש לחוש שיזיק לרבים מתרין בו שלא יעשה ואם אינו משגיח יכולין למסרו וכו',...ונבוא לנד"ד, דפשיטא דבנוסע במהירות מופרזת אשר לא יוכל לעצור את הרכב ברגע שיצטרך לעצור מבלי לגרום אסון, שהזכיר כ"מ במכתבו, דהרי אף בהרבה פחות מזה...., ואם אחרי ההתראה והאזהרה הוא ממשיך כרצונו, מותר למוסרו לשלטונות, - וכמו כן פשיטא במה שנזכר עוד במכתבו, כגון באינו עוצר הרכב בשעה שמסומן עבורו, שיוכלו הולכי רגל לעבור הכביש, וכן ברכב הבא מכוון אחר לנסוע, או שעוקף רכב אחר בצורה המסוכנת, - או שנוהג רכב מבלי שעבר את הבחינה שיודע לנהוג ברכב ולשלוט עליו בעת הצורך - דכל אלו בכלל רודף המסכן עצמו ואחרים, ואף אם אין כוונתו לסכן הוי בכלל רודף כנ"ל. וגם בכלל, אם מעמיד את רכבו בצורה המסכנת את

Responsa & comments of Gedolim

הולכי רגל, או על המדרכה שמאלץ את הולכי הרגל לרדת על פני הכביש שזה מקום מיועד עבור נסיעת כלי רכב ומסוכן עבור הולכי רגל וכיב"ז שהזכיר במכתבו, כל אלה יש להם דין כמו חופר ברה"ר...אמנם כמבואר בש"ע בכל אלו הדינים בין ברודף /חו"מ/ (בסי' תכ"ה) ובין במוסר /חו"מ/ (סי' שפ"ח סעי' י') ובין בעוסק בזיופים שם (סע" י"ב) ובשאר מקומות, דקודם שימסור אותו לערכאות צריכים התראה, כן בנד"ד אין לעשותו מעשה בלא התראת ב"ד, ובכן יש להעסקנים במצוה זו של הצלת נפשות לבוא לפני ב"ד ולהציע הצעתם לפניהם, ויה"ר שחפץ ד' בידכם יצליח וכאשר יצא דבר הב"ד יסכימו ג"כ מן השמים לטובת ותקנת הרבים.

10 מועד קטן (טז.): ומנלן דכפתינן ואסרינן ועבדינן הרדפה - דכתיב (עזרא ז:כו) הן למות הן לשרושי הן לענש נכסין ולאסורין.

11 ר' משה הלברשטאם (מסירה לשלטונות במי שמתעולל בילדיו ע״י תרנא): אם נבוא לדון בדבר השאלה הבאה בזה, באיש רע מעללים שיצרו אונסו לחטוא ולהרשיע, ונתן למוסרו לשלטונות כדי שיצרוהו בתפיסה לכמה שנים עדי ירגיע עצמו וישוב אל ד' בכל ליבו. הנה ע"פ המורם מכל הנ"ל אין כל חטא ופשע במסירה זו. ואדרבה, מצוה היא זו, שבכך גורמים שימנע מלעשות מעשיו המגונים בשנית. דהרי אין לחוש שהשלטונות יענישוהו כמיתה, וכל עיקר העונש שיושת עליו הוא, שיושיבוהו לכמה שנים בבית הסוהר, ויוכל להרוויח בכך שיצמידו לו פסיכולוג או פסיכיאטער שישגיח עליו ועל תהלוכותיו בעינא פקיחא, ואולי יוכל למצוא מזור לנפשו הנאבקת והנאנקת ע"י הטיפול הפסיכולוגי, הנה בכה"ג פשוט הדבר שיפה שעה אחת קודם להצלתו ולהצלת משפחתו

12 ר' משה הלברשטאם (מסירה לשלטונות במי שמתעולל בילדיו ע״י תרנא): כסניף לכל האמור יש להוסיף המובא בשו"ת שבט הלוי (ד:קכ"ד.ג) אשר שאול נשאל מו"ר הגואן האמיתי מרן בעל שבה"ל שליט"א בדבר גזלן מפורסם המתחנן על נפשו שישתדלו להוציאו מבית האסורים, האם שפיר ליעבד הכי. ומשיב דמאחר שאין הגזלן בסכנת נפשות בהיותו בידי השלטונות אין חיוב לעשות השתדלות לאנשים כאלה. ולדידי נראה שלא די שאין חיוב לעשות השתדלות בכגון דא, אלא המשתדל להוציא הגזלן מבית האסורים עוון בידו, ומי לידינו יתקע שלא יתנקם במפליליו, או עכ"פ ישוב לסורו במהרה, ומאן יימר באיזה אופנים שונים יסתימו עלילותיו שלאחר מכן, ואשר על כן יש איסור בדבר להשתדל בעדו ולחוננו....ועכ"פ בהא נחתינן ובהא מסיקינן שהמזדרד למנוע מהאב או מבני המשפחה מלחטוא, בכל אופן שימצא לנכון ואף למוסרו לשלטונות, למצוה יחשב לו. ודבר זה צריך שיהי' בהשכל ודעת, ולא ח"ו בפרסום או בגלוי וכדו'. בכדי שלא יגרם נזק לשאר בני המשפחה, כי אלו הצאן מה חטאו ומה פשעו. וכמאמר המלך שלמה [משלי י"א:ב], את צנועים חכמה.

13 ר' משה הלברשטאם (מסירה לשלטונות במי שמתעולל בילדיו): ... היודע באדם מסויים שהוא חוטא ומרשיע עם יו"ח ברגעים אלו ממש, הרי הוא מחוייב להציל עשוק מיד עושקו ולפנות אל השלטונות תיכף ומיד שיאסרוהו בכבלי ברזל, וינחוהו בבית האסורים לפרק זמן ממושך עד אשר ישכיל להשקיט ולהכניע יצרו, ובאופן שלא יהיה כל חשש שמא יעסוק במעשים מגונים אלו בשנית. ואולם אם אינו חוטא ומרשיע עתה ממש, אך הדברים ידועים שהוא עושה כן, הרי שמלכתחילה טוב ויפה להתרות בו, ואם שומע או יודע שהוא יגע בקצה ציפורנו בא' מיו"ח לטוב או למוטב, כי אז אחת דתו להיות מיושבי בית הכלא לחודשים ושנים רבים. ואולם אין התראה זו לעיכובא כלל וכלל. ע"פ המבואר לעיל ברמ"א ובש"ך, ולפיכך כאשר אין אפשרות להתרות בו, ניתן לפנות אל השלטונות מיד כמבואר לעיל.

Child & Domestic Abuse

14 רמב"ם (הלכות חובל ומזיק ח:יא): ...וכן כל המיצר לציבור ומצער אותן מסרו ביד גוים להכותו ולאסרו ולקנסו, אבל מפני צער יחיד אסור למסרו, ואסור לאבד ממונו של מסור ואע"פ שמותר לאבד גופו שהרי גופו ראוי ליורשיו.

15 רמב"ם (סנהדרין כד:ח-ט): וכן יש לדיין לעשות מריבה עם הראוי לריב עמו ולקללו ולהכותו ולתלוש שערו ולהשביע באלהים בעל כרחו שלא יעשה או שלא עשה... וכן יש לו לכפות ידים ורגלים ולאסור בבית האסורים ולדחוף ולסחוב על הארץ שנאמר הן למות הן לשרושי הן לענש נכסין ולאסורין.

16 ר' יוסף שלום אלישיב (דברי סיני - ירושלים תש"ס ע' מה-מו): שאלה: ממשרד המועצה הדתית במקומנו נגנב מהקופה פעמים אחדות כסף מזומן. לפי כל הסימנים יד אחד מהעובדים בזה, אולם אין בידינו האמצעים שישביאו לידי הודאתו. נשאלת השאלה אם מותר לפנות למשטרה אשר אחרי חקירתה, אם תצליח, תביא את החשוד למשפט החיתוני. המסקנות עלולות להיות חמורות, כי עלול שהחשוד הוא בעל משפחה גדולה. נוסף לכך אם זה מישהו שקשור עם עבודת הקודש, עלול להיות חלילה חילול ה', ר"ל. מאדך גיסא, יתכן שכספי ציבור נעלמים ומי יודע מה עוד. **תשובה:** עיין בשו"ת פנים מאירות ח"ב ס" קנה, מ"ש בנידונו בא' שמצא תיבה פרוצה ונגנב מתוכה הון רב, ויש לו אומדנות המוכיחות שאחד ממשרתיו עשה את המעשה הזה, אי שרי לי' למוסרו לערכאות, ע"פ אומדן יצעו שיודה באמת. והביא שם מעשה רב מהבאון העשל והש"ך, עי"ש. אלא שבסוף הוא מסיק "וחזינן אני מאד שלא למוסרו לערכאותיהם, וכבר אמרו רז"ל כתוא מכמר, יש לחוש שאם יודה, ידונו אותו למיתה." ומכאן דזה לא שייך בזמננו. הרי מן הדין ראשים לפנות למשטרה, אולם לפי"כ כת"ר עלול להיות חילול השם. ואין בידי להביע דעה ע"ז, הואיל ואיני יודע את העניין, והדבר נתון אפוא לשיקול דעת כת"ר.

17 ר' שלמה זלמן אויירבך (ועלהו לא יבול ח"ב עמ' קיג-קיד): ר' יודה גולדרייך אמר שנשאל בדבר יהודי שגנב סכומי כסף גדולים, נתפס על ידי המשטרה בארה"ב ונידון לכמה שנות מאסר — אם ראוי לקיים מצות פדיון שבויים ע"י איסוף סכום כסף גדול (200000 דולאר). הרשז"א השיב: "פדיון שבויים?! פדיון שבויים זה כאשר הגויים תופסים יהודי, סתם, ללא סיבה מוצדקת, ומכניסים אותו לבית הסוהר. לפי מה שידוע לי, בארה"ב לא תופסים סתם כך יהודים כדי לסחוט מהם כסף. הרי התורה אמרת "לא תגנוב", והוא גנב כסף — אדרבה, טוב שישב קצת בכלא וילמד שאסור לגנוב!"

18 ר' יהודה סילמן (ישורון חלק טו עמוד תרע"ג): ב) ולענין למוסרו לשלטון, הרי אם המצב שסגי בפיטורים ואין לחוש שימשיך לפגוע, יש לעשות כן ולא למוסרו. ג) אבל אם יש חשש שהפגיעות ימשכו, הרי, עכ"פ משום לאפרושי מאיסורא, אפשר לדווח, ואף שאם אין זה ג"ע ממש, אין בזה דין רודף, אבל הרי בזמנינו אין כך במאסר שלהם דין פ"נ, ואפשר לעשות כן. ד) ומיהו אין למסור ההחלטה בזה לכל אדם, אלא כמ"ש רש"ל לדיין או לאדם חשוב. ה) וכל הדברים נראים יש לעשות כן, גם ע"פ עדות קטנים או הוכחות אחרות המעוררות חשד סביר וכמו הקלטות, מכתבים או בידקה בפוליגרף, ובלא"ה בדרך כלל אם לא תהא הוכחה, גם בדיניהם לא יענש, ולענין זה א"צ הוכחה גמורה. ו) ואמנם אם החשוד, מוכן לקבל טיפול שיגמול אותו, ובכלל זה, גם טיפול פסיכולוגי, וגם לפי הצורך תרופות שידכאו אצלו את היצר, אם הדבר נראה לפי ראות עיני הדיין שיעשה מה שהבטיח. [ולפעמים לפי ראות עיניו בערבויות מתאימות.] יש להעדיף דרך זו על דיווח, ובתנאי שעכ"פ יפסיק עבודתו. ז) ובחו"ל במקום ששייך דינא דמלכותא, ישנה סיבה נוספת להקל. ח) ומן הראוי לקבוע דיין או ב"ד קבוע שיחליט בכל הנ"ל ולבחור לצורך זה, אנשים עם נסיון בבעיות אלו, מפני חשיבות הנושא הדורשת התמחות מיוחדת.

Responsa & comments of Gedolim

רב שטרנבוך (תשובות והנהגות א:תתן): שאלה: נהג יהודי הרגיל לנסוע במהירות מופרזת או בלי רשיון אם מותר[19] למוסרו למשטרה. מפורש בשולחן ערוך (חושן משפט שפח:יב) שאם עוסק בזיופים ומסוכן מזהירים אותו, ואם אינו משגיח לאזהרה יכולים למוסרו, ע"ש בתיאור הגר"א שיש לו דין רודף אף שאינו מתכוין ואף שאינו רק גרמא ואע"פ שאינו אלא חששא ע"ש, ואין לך מסוכן כמו הנוסע תכופות במהירות מופרזת או בלי ידיעת מלאכת הנהיגה כראוי שלכן לא השיג רשיון, שאלו עלולים להרוג ח"ו ודינם כרודף, לכן התקנה של נהיגה כראוי וברשיון היא בצדק ובישר ולטובת הציבור וחייבין לשמור תקנות אלו, ואם הוא מזלזל בהם ויש חשש שיבוא לאבד נפשות ראוי הוא לעונש מרתיע אף מאסר, ועיין תשב"ץ (ח"ג סימן קס"ח) לאוסרו על ידי נכרים, ובמהרשד"ם ח"מ נה.ו) אמנם כדאי לא למוסרו מיד אלא להתרותו תחילה ע"י רב או העיר או הבית דין שאם ימשיך בדרכו ימסרו אותו למשטרה ולענש כראוי לו, (שבהתראה סתם אינו מאמין שבאמת ימסרוהו), ואם ככל זאת מתעקש בדרכו ומזלזל בציבור, ימסרוהו. (ומרן הגאון רבי יעקב קניבסקי זצ"ל רגז מאד על אלו העוברים חוקי תנועה, שנוסדו לפיקוח נפש דציבור, ושמעתי על אחד שבא לפניו שחושש מאד שיקבל עונש חמור על שעבר על חוקי התנועה ורוצה לבקש ברכתו שיפטרו אותו, והגיב במחאה חריפה מאד, שהאמת שראוי לעונש !) (אף שלא היה ניחא לו במשפטיהם). וע"כ נראה שאם הוא בגדר מועד ואי אפשר לנו להעניש בעצמנו ועלול להזיק, ראוי ברשות בית דין או רב העיר למוסרו ומצוה קעביד להציל את הציבור ממזיק שעלול לסכן אפילו לסכן את חייהם.

ר' משה הלברשטאם (מסירה לשלטונות במי שמתעולל בילדיו ע' תרנא): כסניף לכל האמור יש להוסיף המובא בשו"ת[20] שבט הלוי (ד:קכד.ג) אשר שאול נשאל מו"ר הגאון האמיתי מרן בעל שבה"ל שליט"א בדבר גזלן מפורסם המתחנן על נפשו שישתדלו להוציאו מבית האסורים, האם שפיר ליעבד הכי. ומשיב דמאחר שאין הגזלן בסכנת נפשות בהיותו בידי השלטונות אין חיוב לעשות השתדלות לאנשים כאלה. ולדידי נראה שלא די שאין חיוב לעשות השתדלות בכגון דא, אלא המשתדל להוציא הגזלן מבית האסורים עוון בידו, ומי לידינו יתקע שלא יתנקם במפליליו, או עכ"פ ישוב לסורו במהרה, ומאן יימר באיזה אופנים שונים יסתיימו עלילותיו שלאחר מכן, ואשר על כן איסור יש בדבר להשתדל בעדו ולחוננו....ועכ"פ בהא נחתינן ובהא מסיקנן שהמזודרז למנוע מהאב או מבני המשפחה מלחטוא, בכל אופן שימצא לנכון ואף למוסרו לשלטונות, למצוה יחשב לו. ודבר זה צריך שיהי' בהשכל ודעת, ולא ח"ו בפרסום או בגלוי וכד'. בכדי שלא יגרום נזק לשאר בני המשפחה, כי אלו הצאן מה חטאו ומה פשעו. וכמאמר המלך שלמה [משלי יא:ב], את צנועים חכמה.

שבט הלוי (ד:קכד.ג): ועל אשר שאל בגזלן מפורסם שגזל לאנשים הרבה, וממש בצורת גזלן והוא מזיק הרבים ומתחנן[21] להוציאו מבית הסורה האם שפיר למיעבד הכי - וכ"ת העיר משי"ד סי' קנ"ח ס"ק ג' ובמה שהעיר עליו בס' מקור חיים - ובאמת המעיין [ועיין בתשובת חוות יאיר סי' קל"ט והובא בקיצור גם בפת"ש יו"ד סי' רנ"א] בשו"ע חו"מ סי' שפ"ח ברמ"א סי"א, ובבאר הגולה שם שכ' וכבר פשט התיקון והמנהג שלא לעשות שקר ועולה לאומות ומכריזין ונותנין רשות לפרסם ולגלות על האנשים אשר לוקחים בהקפה וכו' וכן בשו"ע חו"מ סי' תכ"ה ברמ"א סוס"א - בכל אלה מקומות יראה שאין חשש כלל להניחם כך כדי שלא יזיק כיון שאינו בסכנת נפש בידיהם - דהחוות יאיר שם כ' רק כשהי' בסכנת נפש ממש - ועיין בתשובת מהר"ם אלשיך סו"ס ס"ו - ובי"ד סי' קנ"ז סו"ס א' ובפת"ש שם ס"ק י"ג, וכבר הארכתי מעין ובדומה לזה בעניי בתשובת שבט הלוי יו"ד סי' נ"ח - ודעתי העני' שכל זמן שאין סכנת נפשות אין חיוב לעשות השתדלות לאנשים כאלה, ויצרף עוד דעת תורה בזה - מחמת אפס הזמן אקצר הרני דוש"ת באהבה, +ע"ע ח"ה סי' קל"ה+

Child & Domestic Abuse

22 **ר' יוסף שלום אלישיב (דברי סיני - ירושלים תש"ס ע' מה-מו): שאלה**: ממשרד המועצה הדתית במקומנו נגנב מהקופה פעמים אחדות כסף מזומן. לפי כל הסימנים יד אחד מהעובדים בזה, אולם אין בידינו האמצעים שיביאו לידי הודאתו. נשאלת השאלה אם מותר לפנות למשטרה אשר אחרי חקירתה, תביא את החשוד למשפט החיתוני. המסקנות עלולות להיות חמורות, כי עלול שהחשוד הוא בעל מפשחה גדולה. נוסף לכך אם זה מישהו שקשור עם עבודת הקודש, עלול להיות חלילה גם חילול ה', ר"ל. מאדך גיסא, יתכן שכספי ציבור נעלמים ומי יודע מה עוד. **תשובה**: עיין בשו"ת פנים מאירות ח"ב סי' קנה, מ"ש בנידונו בא' שמצא תיבה פרוצה ונגנב מתוכה הון רב, ויש לו אומדנות המוכיחות שאחד ממשרתיו עשה את המעשה הזה, אי שרי לי' למוסרו לערכאות, ע"פ אומדן יעצו שיודה באמת. והביא שם מעשה רב מהבאון העשל והש"ך, עי"ש. אלא שבסוף הוא מסיק "וחכך אני מאוד שלא למוסרו לערכאותיהם, וכבר אמרו רז"ל כתוא מכמר, יש לחוש שאם יודה, ידונו אותו למיתה." ומכאן דזה לא שייך בזמננו. הרי מן הדין ראשים לפנות למשטרה, אולם לפי"ד כת"ר עלול להיות חילול השם. ואין בידי להביע דעה ע"ז, הואיל ואיני יודע את העניין, והדבר נתון אפוא לשיקול דעת כת"ר.

23 **ר' משה הלברשטאם (מסירה לשלטונות במי שמתעולל בילדיו ע' תרנא)**: כסניף לכל האמור יש להוסיף המובא בשו"ת שבט הלוי (ד:קכד.ג) אשר שאול נשאל מו"ר הגאון האמיתי מרן בעל שבה"ל שליט"א בדבר גזלן מפורסם המתחנן על נפשו שישתדלו להוציאו מבית האסורים, האם שפיר ליעבד הכי. ומשיב דמאחר שאין הגזלן בסכנת נפשות בהיותו בידי השלטונות אין חיוב לעשות השתדלות לאנשים כאלה. ולדידי נראה שלא די שאין חיוב לעשות השתדלות בכגון דא, אלא המשתדל להוציא הגזלן מבית האסורים עוון בידו, ומי לידינו יתקע שלא יתנקם במפליליו, או עכ"פ ישוב לסורו במהרה, ומאן יימר באיזה אופנים שונים יסתימו עלילותיו שלאחר מכן, ואשר על כן יש איסור בדבר להשתדל בעדו ולחוננו...ועכ"פ בהא נחתינן ובהא מסיקנן שהמהדרר למנוע מהאב או מבני המשפחה מלחטוא, בכל אופן שימצא לנכון ואף למוסרו לשלטונות, למצוה יחשב לו. ודבר זה צריך שיהי' בהשכל ודעת, ולא ח"ו בפרסום או בגלוי וכדו'. בכדי שלא יגרם נזק לשאר בני המשפחה, כי אלו הצאן מה חטאו ומה פשעו. וכמאמר המלך שלמה [משלי י"א:ב], את צנועים חכמה.

24 **ר' יהודה סילמן (ישורון חלק טו עמוד תרע"ג)**: ב) ולעניין למוסרו לשלטון, הרי אם המצב שסגי בפיטורים ואין לחוש שימשיך לפגוע, יש לעשות כן ולא למוסרו. ג) אבל אם יש חשש שהפגיעות ימשכו, הרי, עכ"פ משום לאפרושי מאיסורא, אפשר לדווח, ואף שאם אין זה ג"ע ממש, אין בזה דין רודף, אבל הרי בזמנינו בין כך אין במאסר שלהם דין פ"נ, ואפשר לעשות כן. ד) ומיהו אין למסור ההחלטה בזה לכל אדם, אלא כמ"ש רש"ל לדיין או לאדם חשוב. ה) וכל הדברים נראים לעשות כן, גם ע"פ עדות קטנים או הוכחות אחרות המעוררות חשד סביר וכמו הקלטות, מכתבים או בידקה בפוליגרף, ובלא"ה בדרך כלל אין זו תהא הוכחה, גם בדיניהם לא יענש, ולעניין זה א"צ הוכחה גמורה. ו) ואמנם אם החשוד, מוכן לקבל טיפול שיגמול אותו, ובכלל זה, גם טיפול פסיכולוגי, וגם לפי הצורך תרופות שידכאו אצלו את היצר, אם הדבר נראה לפי ראות עיני הדיין שיעשה מה שהבטיח. [ולפעמים לפי ראות עיניו בערבויות מתאימות.] יש להעדיף דרך זו על דיווח, ובתנאי שעכ"פ יפסיק עבודתו. ז) ובחו"ל במקום ששייך דינא דמלכותא, ישנה סיבה נוספת להקל. ח) ומן הראוי לקבוע דיין או ב"ד קבוע שיחליט בכל הנ"ל ולבחור לצורך זה, אנשים עם נסיון בבעיות אלו, מפני חשיבות הנושא הדורשת התמחות מיוחדת.

Responsa & comments of Gedolim

שבט הלוי (ד:קכד.ג): ועל אשר שאל בגזלן מפורסם שגזל לאנשים הרבה, וממש בצורת גזלן והוא מזיק הרבים ומתחנן [25] להוציאו מבית הסוהר האם שפיר למיעבד הכי - וכ"ת העיר משו"ך יו"ד סי' קנ"ח ס"ק ג' ובמה שהעיר עליו בס' מקור חיים - ובאמת המעיין [ועיין בתשובת חוות יאיר סי' קל"ז והובה בקיצור גם בפתח"ש יו"ד סי' רנ"א] בשו"ע חו"מ סי' שפ"ח ברמ"א סי"א, ובבאר הגולה שם שכ' וכבר פשט התיקון והמנהג שלא לעשות שקר ועולה לאומות ומכריזין ונותנים רשות לפרסם ולגלות על האנשים אשר לוקחים בהקפה וכו' וכן בשו"ע חו"מ סי' תכ"ה ברמ"א סוס"א - בכל אלה מקומות יראה שאין חשש כלל להניחו כך כדי שלא יזיק כיון שאינו בסכנת נפש בידיהם - דהחוות יאיר שם כ' רק כשהי' בסכנת נפש ממש - ועיין בתשובת מהר"ם אלשיך סו"ס ס"ו - וביו"ד סי' קנ"ז סו"ס א' ובפת"ש שם ס"ק י"ג, וכבר הארכתי מעין ובדומה לזה בעניי בתשובת שבט הלוי יו"ד סי' נ"ח - ודעתי העני' שכל זמן שאין סכנת נפשות אין חיוב לעשות השתדלות לאנשים כאלה, ויצרף עוד דעת תורה בזה - מחמת אפס הזמן אקצר הרני דוש"ת באהבה, +ע"ח"ה סי' קל"ה+

ר' יהודה סילמן (ישורון חלק טו): מאמר נספה: בדין ספק רודף - אי מותר להורגו נשאלתי, מאבטח במקום ציבורי - [26] פתח מסעדה, קנינו וכו' שמבחין באדם שמתקרב ונראה חשוד - והוא מתנהג כצורה מוזרה, ונראה כערבי, ופונים אליו והוא מתחיל לברוח וכל כה"ג, והוא חושד שמא הוא מחבל - והנה אין זה ברור דאפשר שהוא יהודי ויש בעולם אנשים מוזרים, וגם הבריחה יכולה להיות תגובה של פחד. אבל יתכן שבעוד שתי דקות יעשה פיגוע גדול. האם עליו להורגו מספק.

שאלה שניה: וכעין זה יש לשאול פקיד כבנק, שפורץ לשם שודד שאקדח בידו. ולעיתים קרובות מתברר שזה רק אקדח צעצוע. דאף אם הוא אמיתי אין כוונתו להרוג אלא לאיים אבל מכלל ספק לא נפיק האם מותר להורגו.

תשובה: ...דינים העולים בדין ספק רודף א) נראה דיש לנקוט לדינא שמותר להרוג ספק רודף, והיינו מי שעושה פעולה המסכנת אחרים אף מספק. ונראה שדין דה מבואר ברמ"א ב) ואם הוא רודף אחרי אסופי, ספק ישראל תפק גרי, ג"כ שרי [מנחת חינוך] וכן נראה דמוכח מתשובת רדב"ז.ג.) ואם יש רוב שאינו ישראל, המנחת חינון התיר גם בזה להרגו, ויש לדון בזה. ד) ולפ"ז בשני אופני השאלה הנ"ל באדם חשוד יש להתיר הריגתו. והיינו כל מקום אמיתי להסתפק. ה) אמנם הרץ ביער או יורה ויש ספק בכוונתו. אין לדונו כרודף, דסתמא יש לו חזקת כשרית.

חתם סופר (גיטין ז.): בני אדם העומדים עלי פירש"י לחרף ולגדף... וא"כ לא עמדו עליו אלא לחרפו ואפ"ה אי לאו [27] דיכול להציל עצמו ע"י השכמת בהמ"ד היה רשאי למסרו למלכות כמדקרת חרב אבל מדפירש"י אקרא בעוד רשע לנגדי מריבני ומקניטני מוכח דפשיטא לי' לרש"י מצערי' דאלו הי' מצערי' בממון וזיוף מותר למסרו ואינו צריך להשכים ולהשכים כי הבא להרגך השכם להרגו וכן פסק הרמב"ם (מחובל ומזיק ט:יא) בסופו וכן המיצר ומצער הצבור מותר למסרו ביד גוי להכותו וכו' אבל מפני צער יחיד אסור למסרו וכו' משמע מיצרו מצער בעלמא אבל מפסידו מותר למסרו שלא יפסדנו עוד כמ"ש רמ"א (חשון משפט שפח:ט) וכ"כ ש"ך (חשון משפט שפח:נט-ס). אך מאי דפשיטא לרמב"ם דבמצער ציבור מותר למסרו נושאי כליו לא הראו מקום כליי לא דין זה. וצ"ל דמשמע מסוגיין דאי לאו דהוה לי' הצלה ע"י השכם והערב היה מותר למסרו וזה מותר שייך ליעצמו ביחיד אבל בציבור קדירא דבי שותפא מי יערב וישכים בעד כולם ע"כ מותר למוסרו. וע"י פני' בשקלא וטריא דשמעתין דדברי א"ח המה ונלמד ממנו אפי' להשכים למסור לעריב דינו לשמים נמי אינו נכון אפי' אין לו דין למטה כל זמן דמצי למיקם בהו ולא יבלום פיו בשעת מריבה אא"כ לא מצי למיקם בהו אז מותר להשכים ולהעריב עליהם ואי הם גורמים לו דמחמת צערו יש לו ביטול תורה ותפלה מותר בכל כי א"א

Child & Domestic Abuse

להשכים ולהעריב וזה שאמר דהע"ה החשיתי מטוב שלא יכולתי להשכים ולהעריב ע"כ דברתי בלשוני זהו היוצא לנו מדברי פנ"י ז"ל:

[28] פתחי תשובה (אורח חיים סימן קנו): ...וראיתי להזכיר פה ע"ד אשר כל הספרי מוסר הרעישו העולם על עון לה"ר ואנכי מרעיש העולם להיפוך עון גדול מזה וגם הוא מצוי יותר והוא מניעת עצמו מלדבר במקום הנצרך להציל את העשוק מיד עושקו. דרך משל במי שראה באחד שהוא אורב על חבירו בערמה על הדרך במדבר להרגו או שראה חותר מחתרת בלילה בביתו או בחנותו היתכן שימנע מלהודיע לחבירו שיזהר ממנו משום איסור לשון הרע הלא עונו גדול מנשוא שעובר על לא תעמוד על דם רעיך. וכן בעני ממון הוא בכלל השבת אבידה. ועתה מה לי חותר מחתרת או שראיתי משרתיו גונבים ממונו בסתר או שותפו גונב דעתו בעסק או שחבירו מטעהו במקח וממכר או שלוה מעות והוא גברא דלאו פרענא הוא. וכן בעיני שידוכי והוא יודע שהוא איש רע ובליעל ורע להתחתן עמו כולן בכלל השבת אבידת גופו וממונו. ועתה איה לנו הגדר והגבול לומר עד פה תדבר ולא יותר. והכלל בזה שהדיבור מסור ללב אם כונתו לרעת האחד לשון הרע הוא אבל אם כונתו לטובת השני להצילו ולשמרו הוא מצוה רבה. וזהו לדעתי עומק כונת הירושלמי שהביא המ"א דמותר לדבר לה"ר על בעלי המחלוקת. ולכאורה קשה ע"ז מהא דאמרינן מ"ק (דף טז) דיליף דבשליח ב"ד אין בו משום לשון הרע מדהגיד משה העיני האנשים ההם תנקר וכו' ומאי ראיה הא עדת קרח ה"ה בעלי המחלוקת. והוא אשר דברתי דודאי גם על בעל מחלוקת אין לספר בחנם רק בדבר המחלוקת שהוא צופה רעת חבירו אז מותר לגלות גנותו להצלת חבירו ולפ"ז מוכח שפיר דמה שאמר לשמה מה שאמרו עדת קרח הוא בלא תועלת וע"כ רק הוא משום דשליח ב"ד מותר שוב מצאתי כן בגליון הש"ס על הירושלמי. ועתה כמה פעמים אנו רואים חבירו תקלת חבירו בהשרשת הפרוסה לרגליהם מאדם רע וכובשים פניו באמרי מה לנו להכניס בדבר אשר אינו נוגע לנו וע"י בתשו' מקום שמואל (סי' צא) אהא דמתאמרי באפי מרא לית ביה משום ל"ב היינו דוקא במתכוין לשם תוכחה אבל לא לקנתור ע"ש. ובדברים כאלו וכי"ב כבר אמרו חז"ל בדבר המסור ללב נאמר ויראת מאלהיך.

[29] רמב"ם (הלכות סנהדרין ב:יב): יש לאדם לעשות דין לעצמו אם יש בידו כח הואיל וכדת וכהלכה הוא עושה אינו חייב לטרוח ולבוא לבית דין, אף על פי שלא היה שם הפסד בנכסיו אילו נתאחר ובא לבית דין, לפיכך אם קבל עליו בעל דינו והביאו לבית דין ודרשו ומצאו שעשה כהלכה ודין אמת דן לעצמו אין סותרין את דינו.

[30] רמב"ם (הלכות חובל ומזיק ח:ט): אסור למסור ישראל ביד גוים בין בגופו בין בממונו ואפילו היה רשע ובעל עבירות ואפילו היה מיצר לו ומצערו וכל המוסר ישראל ביד גוים בין בגופו בין בממונו אין לו חלק לעולם הבא:

[31] רמב"ם (הלכות חובל ומזיק ח:יא): ...וכן כל המיצר לציבור ומצער אותן מותר למסרו ביד גוים להכותו ולאסרו ולקנסו, אבל מפני צער יחיד אסור למסרו, ואסור לאבד ממונו של מסור ואע"פ שמותר לאבד גופו שהרי ממונו ראוי ליורשיו.

[32] רב שטרנבוך (תשובות והנהגות א:תתנ): שאלה: נהג יהודי הרגיל לנסוע במהירות מופרזת או בלי רשיון אם מותר למוסרו למשטרה. **מפורש** בשולחן ערוך (חושן משפט שפח:יב) שאם עוסק בזיופים ומסוכן מזהירים אותו, ואם אינו משגיח לאזהרה יכולים למוסרו, עי"ש בתיאור הגר"א שיש לו דין רודף אף שאינו מתכוין אף שאינו רק גרמא ואע"פ שאינו אלא חששא עי"ש, ואין לך מסוכן כמו הנוסע תכופות במהירות מופרזת או בלי ידיעת מלאכת הנהיגה כראוי שלכן לא השיג רשיון, שאלו עלולים להרוג ח"ו ודינם כרודף, לכן התקנה של נהיגה כראוי וברשיון היא בצדק וביושר ולטובת הציבור וחייבין לשמור תקנות אלו, ואם הוא מזלזל בהם ויש חשש שיבוא לאבד נפשות ראוי הוא לעונש מרתיע אף מאסר, ועיין

Responsa & comments of Gedolim

תשב"ץ (ח"ג סימן קס"ח) לאוסרו על ידי נכרים, ובמהרשד"ם ח"מ נה.ו) אמנם כדאי לא למוסרו מיד אלא להתרותו תחילה ע"י רב העיר או הבית דין שאם ימשיך בדרכו ימסרו אותו למשטרה ולענש כראוי לו, (שבהתראה סתם אינו מאמין שבאמת ימסרוהו), ואם ככל זאת מתעקש בדרכו ומזלזל בציבור, ימסרוהו. (ומרן הגאון רבי יעקב קנייבסקי זצ"ל רגז מאד על אלו העוברים חוקי תנועה, שנוסדו לפיקוח נפש דציבור, ושמעתי על אחד שבא לפניו שחושש מאד שיקבל עונש חמור על שעבר על חוקי התנועה ורוצה לבקש ברכתו שיפטרו אותו, והגיב במחאה חריפה מאד, שהאמת שראוי לענוש!) (אף שלא היה ניחא לו במשפטיהם). וע"כ נראה שאם הוא בגדר מועד ואי אפשר לנו להענישו בעצמנו ועלול להזיק, ראוי ברשות בית דין או רב העיר למוסרו ומצוה קעביד להציל את הציבור ממזיק שעלול אפילו לסכן את חייה.

33 ר' **משה שטרנבוך (ה:שצח שמיעת רינונים וחשדות):** קבלתי מכתבו, וראה אחזתני על פשע המנהל שסירב לשמוע טענות נגד ר"מ על מעשים מגונים, בטענה שזהו לשון הרע, ועכשיו מתגלה והולך קלונו של אותו ר"מ, והמנהל עודו מתעקש שאין הוכחות מספיקות וראוי לחשוש לאיסור לשון הרע.

ודבריו של המנהל הם הבל הבלים, ופותח פתח לשחיתות ר"ל, וחובת ראש ישיבה ומנהל לשמוע כל רינון וחשד על המתרחש בתחומו, שכן עיקר חובתו לשמור על נפשותיהם של התלמידים, ולכן צריך לחשוש לכל דבר אפילו אינו מצוי כלל, ואף שמוקמינן על חזקת כשרותו, מכל מקום מה שנוגע לשמירת התלמידים, אם נראה אפילו נדנוד ספק שהוזקו ילדים או בחורים, חייבין לסלק את החשד בינתיים או להעמיד שמירה מיוחדת ותמידית עליו, ועיקר איסור סיפור וקבלת לשון הרע, הוא אם נוגע מכך ששונאו או מקנא בו ואין כוונתו לש"ש, אבל כשכוונתו טהורה חייב לחשוש לכל טענה וינון או על מנת למנוע נזקים, והחשש המופרז מאיסור לשון הרע עלול לגרום לקלקול רבים.

ופעם אחת כשהייתי אצל כ"ק האדמו"ר רבי ישראל אלתר (האדמו"ר מגור) שאל אותי אודות בחור אחד, וכיון שחששש שאני מפקפק אם להגיד מפני לשון הרע, אמר "דע לך בבית דין בבית אין איסור לשון הרע שהכל לתועלת, וכל מה שאני שומע אני פועל ועושה ובע"ה יהא תמיד בזה תועלת".

והנה שמעתי על אסיפת רבנים בה עמד הקדוש ה"חפץ חיים" זצ"ל ודרש על ענין לשון הרע, ובקש מהרבנים הנוכחים שיחתמו על התחייבות להזהר מלשון הרע, והגאון רבי חיים עוזר זצ"ל היסס לחתום, ויש בזה סיפורים שונים, וכפי ששמעתי השיב שרב בעירו צריך לידע ולשמוע הכל אפילו בחשש רחוק מאד ולעשות בירור אם יש בדברים ממש, ובמדה שיחתום עלול להחמיר מדאי וזה יגרום קלקול לרבים ולכן טוב יותר לתקן ללמוד הלכות לשון הרע.

סוף דבר, מצוה גדולה לספור כל חשש וחשד, והמנהל צריך לשמוע ולחשוש ולשמור על התלמידים שמירה מעולה, ואם מתרשל הרי היא בכלל ארור עושה מלאכת ה' רמיה, והיום יש הרבה כלי משחית לקלקל הנוער, וחובה לשמור שמירה מעולה על קודש הקדשים, התלמידים העוסקים בתורת ה', (כמבואר בלשון הרמב"ם סוף הלכות שמיטה ויובל ע"ש).

ואני באתי לעודדו שלא ינוח ולא ישקוט, ושכרו רב מאד, ויסכר פי דובר שקר הסותם פיות ומזלזל בדברים הנוגעים לדיני נפשות.

34 **נשמת אברהם (ד:רח סי' שפח:א - אסור למסור ע' ר"ז-רי"א):.** ילד או תינוק שהובא לבית חולים עם תסמונת "הילד המוכה", דהיינו עם שברים מרובים בגולגולת או בגפיים, או עם דימומים באברים הפנימיים עקב מכות או בעיטות קשות, או עם כוויית קשות מאש, חשמל או מים רותחים וכו'. שנעשה באכזריות ובמזיד ע"י אחד או שני הוריו. אסור אחרי

Child & Domestic Abuse

הטיפול המושלמים, להזהיר אותו לביתו כי אז ימשיכו להכות בו עד המוות. בגלל סכנת הנפשות הממשית, על הרופא להודיע לבית המשפט ואז ע"י צו בית המשפט מעבירים למשפחה את התינוק אומנת או למוסד. נראה שאין בזה שאלה של מוסר מכיון שמדובר בסכנת נפשות של ממש והורים לדינא דין של רודף, ויתכן שמותר גם אם מעבירים את התינוק, בלית ברירה, למשפחה או למוסד לא דתי. אך כמובן יצטרך בית דין לעשות הכל שביכולתו לדאוג לזה שהילד יועבר למשפחה או למוסד שומר תורה ומצוות. ובמיוחד בחוץ לארץ על הבית דין לדאוג שלא יועבר הילד למשפחה או מוסד של עכו"ם. והסכים אתי הגרש"ז אויערבאך שליט"א.

[35] **שבט הלוי (ב:נח)**: א) באחד שעובד במשרד המכס וכשהוא רואה מי שרימה את הממשלה צריך למסור אותו בבית המשפט ורצונו לדעת אם הוא בגדר מלשין או דינא דמלכותא דינא.

הנה בעצם דין מכס דין ולית דיין שזה נכנס בגדר דינא דמלכותא דינא גם לדעת החולקים בחו"מ סי' שס"ט ס"ח ברמ"א, ועיין בש"ך חו"מ סי' ע"ג ס"ק ל"ט ובלבוש סוסי' שס"ט ובתשובת השיב משה סימן צ' בזה.

ולעניין למסור למלכות הנה מש"ס (ב"מ פג:) בעובדא דר"א בר"ש דהוי מסר גנבא למלכות מוכח דהוא מותר משום הורמנא דמלכא, ואף על גב דאמרו לי' עד מתי אתה מוסר עמו של אלקינו להריגה, היינו משום שנוגע לסכנת נפשות של ישראל וכן מש"כ אלי' זל"ט שם פ"ד ע"א לר' ישמעאל ב"ר יוסי, אבל מעיקר הדין משמע דגם בכזה איכא דין מלכות עיין היטב בריטב"א שבשטמ"ק.

ובבאר הגולה חו"מ סי' שפ"ח, כתב וז"ל וכבר פשט התיקון והמנהג שמנהיגי הקהלות עומדים על המשמר שלא לעשות שקר ועולה לאומות ומכריזים ונותנים רשות לפרסם ולגלות על האנשים אשר לוקחי' בהקפה וכו' יעש"ה ורע"ש ברמ"א סי"א, מי שרוצה לברוח ולא לשלם לעכו"ם מה שחייב לו ואחר גילה לו אין בזה דין מוסר וכו' ואעפ"י שמסיים רמ"א דמ"מ רעה עשה דהוי כמשיב אבדה לעכו"ם היינו משום שמעירי עכו"ם יחידי אבל מה שנוגע למלכות והוא ממונה על כך אין בזה איסור כנ"ל,

אלא דלכתחילה כדאי שלא לקבל משרה כזאת דצריך למסור אפילו בהיתר דלאו משנת חסידים הוא וכדאיתא גם כן בירושלמי סופ"ח דתרומות בכיו"ב, וע"ע בתשובת מהר"ם אלשיך סוסי' ס"ו כ' בכיו"ב דאין בו דין מסור מטעם דינא דמלכותא דינא, ועיין עוד ברמ"א יו"ד סי' קל"ז סוס"א ובפת"ש שם ס"ק י"ג, ועיין היטב בד"ת שם ס"ק נ"ג בשם הב"ח באיזה אופן מותר למסור לכתחילה. וע"ע בפת"ש יו"ד סי' רנ"א מש"כ בשם חוי' סי' קל"ט ועוד, ופשיטא דאינו דומה לנ"ד דהתם מיירי לידי סכנה אם ימסרוהו לגוים משא"כ כשמטילים עליו עונש בעלמא ואינו בא לכלל סכנה לעולם.

[36] **ר' יהודה סילמן (ישורון חלק טו)**: מאמר נספה: בדין ספק רודף - אי מותר להורגו נשאלתי, מאבטח במקום ציבורי - פתח מסעדה, קניון וכו' שמבחין באדם שמתקרב ונראה חשוד - והוא מתנהג כצורה מוזרה, ונראה כערבי, ופונים אליו והוא מתחיל לברוח וכל כה"ג, והוא חושד שמא הוא מחבל - והנה אין זה ברור דאפשר שהוא יהודי ויש בעולם אנשים מוזרים, וגם הבריחה יכולה להיות תגובה של פחד. אבל יתכן שבעוד שתי דקות יעשה פיגוע גדול. האם עליו להורגו מספק.

שאלה שניה: וכעין זה יש לשאול פקיד כבנק, שפורץ לשם שודד שאקדח בידו. ולעיתים קרובות מתברר שזה רק אקדח צעצוע. דאף אם הוא אמיתי אין כוונתו להרוג אלא לאיים אבל מכלל ספק לא נפיק האם מותר להורגו.

136

Responsa & comments of Gedolim

תשובה: ...דינים העולים בדין ספק רודף א) נראה דיש לנקוט לדינא שמותר להרוג ספק רודף, והיינו מי שעושה פעולה המסכנת אחרים אף מספק. ונראה שדין דה מבואר ברמ"א ב) ואם הוא רודף אחרי אסופי, ספק ישראל ספק גרי, ג"כ שרי [מנחת חינוך] וכן נראה דמוכח מתשובת רדב"ז.ג) ואם יש רוב שאינו ישראל, המנחת חינוך התיר גם בזה להרוג, ויש לדון בזה. ד) ולפ"ז בשני אופני השאלה הנ"ל באדם חשוד יש להתיר הריגתו. והיינו כל מקום אמיתי להסתפק. ה) אמנם הרץ ביער או יורה ויש ספק בכוונתו, אין לדונו כרודף, דסתמא יש לו חזקת כשרית.

37 ר' יהודה סילמן (ישורון חלק טו עמוד תרס"ב) ... ה) והנה פשוט שא"צ בכל זה לעדים וכלשון הגמ' ב"מ (פג) לתפוס מי ששתי חמרא והוא מנמנם, ואח"כ אמר ראב"ש, מה ספיקות שלכם כן ודאי על אחת כמה וכמה, כאשר פירש"י שודאי היינו במקום שיש טעם הגון כמו הטעם הנ"ל, ומ' שסמם גם על פחות מזה, והטעם פשוט שאין זה עונש מדין ב"ד, אלא או משום חוק המלכות או לאפרושי מאיסורא, ובת' הרשב"א בב"י שם במוארר שא"צ עדים וז"ל, ואיזהו מוחזק כל שנודע לרבים שהוא כן, לא שהוחזק בב"ד של כ"ג, ושקיבלו עידיו בפניו, וכל שהשעה צריכה כך מכין ועונשין שלא מן הדין בכל מקום ובכל זמן כהדוא שרכב על סוס בשבת [ומבואר דהנידון בכח הכפיה של ישראל ולא בח המלכות] וסיים שא"צ קבלת עדים בפניו, שאין הולכין בכל אלו אלא אחר ידיעת האמת לסלק הניזוק ולעשות גדרים בפני פרצות, ולטעם שכתבנו שספק רודף שרי, פשוט דשרי בכה"ג דסגי נהיה לנו ספק.

38 ר' יהודה סילמן (ישורון חלק טו עמוד תרע"ג): דינים העולים. יש כאן שני נידונים נפרדים א) לענין לפטרו מעבודה, בזה קי"ל זה כדעת השו"מ שסגי בייצא עליו שם רע. דיש לחוש מספק. ונ' דבכה"ג שיש רגלים לדבר, אפשר לפטרו באמצע השנה, וגם אין מגיע לו פיצויים. ב) ולענין למוסרו לשלטון, הרי אם המצב שסגי בפיטורים ואין לחוש שימשיך לפגוע, יש לעשות כן ולא למוסרו. ג) אבל אם יש חשש שהפגיעות ימשכו, הרי, עכ"פ משום לאפרושי מיאסורא, אפשר לדווח, ואף שאם אין זה ג"ע ממש, אין בזה דין רודף, אבל הרי בזמנינו בין כך אין במאסר שלהם דין פ"נ, ואפשר לעשות כן. ד) ומיהו אין למסור ההחלטה בזה לכל אדם, אלא כמ"ש רש"ל לדיין או לאדם חשוב. ה) וכל הדברים נראים יש לעשותם כן, גם ע"פ עדות קטינים או הוכחות אחרות המעוררות חשד סביר וכמו הקלטות, מכתבים או בידקה בפוליגרף, ובלא"ה בדרך כלל אם לא תהא הוכחה, גם בדיניהם לא יענש, ולענין זה א"צ הוכחה גמורה. ו) ואמנם אם החשוד, מוכן לקבל טיפול שיגמול אותו, ובכלל זה, גם טיפול פסיכולוגי, וגם לפי הצורך תרופות שידכאו אצלו את היצר, אם הדבר נראה לפי ראות עיני הדיין שיעשה מה שהבטיח. [ולפעמים לפי ראות עיניו בערבויות מתאימות.] יש להעדיף דרך זו על דיווח, ובתנאי שעכ"פ יפסיק עבודתו. ז) ובחו"ל במקום ששייך דינא דמלכותא, ישנה סיבה נוספת להקל. ח) ומן הראוי לקבוע דיין או ב"ד קבוע שיחליט בכל הנ"ל ולבחור לצורך זה, אנשים עם נסיון בבעיות אלו, מפני חשיבות הנושא הדורשת התמחות מיוחדת.

39 ר' יהודה סילמן (ישורון חלק כב ע' תקפט-תקצ): ב) לשאלה השניה אם ניתן לחייב את הפוגע בתשלום כלשהו משורת הדין, למעשה מה שיש לדון בו במקרים כאלו הוא בעיקר משום ריפוי, ז"א הוצאות הטיפול פיכולוגי הנצרך, כי מה שהתספק רב גדול אחד שליט"א שמא אין זה בכלל ריפוי, הואיל ולפי ניסוינו הנופלים קרבן להתעללות כזו בימי ילדותם ובחרותם כמעט ואין תרופה למכתם בעצם, ובורב המקרים כל הטיפולים שהם עוברים במשך השנים אינם מרפאיסאותם, רק עוזרים להם ומלמדתם להתמודד עד כמה שאפשר עם בעיותיהם – לא ניחא לי, שהמציאות היא שבחלק גדול מהמקרים הוא מתרפא לגמרי, וכמעט בכולם עכ"פ יש תועלת בריפוי, שלכן פשוט לע"ד שאף זה בכלל ריפוי, והגע בעצמך, החובל

Child & Domestic Abuse

באם ואין רפואה למכתו, וכתוצאה מחבלתו הוא זקוק לתרופות וטיפולים משך כל ימי חייו, היעלה על הדעת שלאו ריפוי הוא זה, אתמההה??

אלא שלכאורה התינה לבני עות המזרח הנוקטים כשיטת המחבר (ח.מ. סי' א' ס"ב) שב"ד דן וגובה שבת וריפוי בזה"ז, אבל אנן לדידן נקטינן הרי ברמ"א (ח"מ סי' א' ס"ב) שאין דנים וגובים בזה"ז. ברם, אי משום הא לא איריא, דעיי"ש רמ"א שממשיך ומסיק: "כופין החובל לפייס הנחבל ולקנסו כפי הנראה להם (פי' לב"ד), וכמו שיבואר בסמוך סעיף ה". ומה שציין לסי' ה, כוונתו לדברי המחבר שם: "אעפ"י שדיינים שאינם סמוכים בא"י אינם מגבין קנסות, מנדין אותו, עד שיפייס לבעל דינו: וכיון שיתן לו שיעור הראוי לו, מתירין לו" – וכים שאין דרך לנדות, העצה היעוצה היא ללחוץ עליו בפרסום הרחקה שעושים במקום שהיה חייב נידוי, ובמקרה שהוא תחם על שטר בוררות הכולל זכות לדיין לפסוק ליפ יושר, אפשר לחייבו אף ממון. ג) גם נראה לי לנכון הצעת רב אחד שליט"א, שבמקרים של התקשרות בין הצדדים, כגון מלמדים והדומה (שרוב מקרי התעללות הם במצבים כאלו), יש להכניס סעיף מפורש בהסכם ההתקשרות בין הצדדים, ולפיו הוא מתחייב לשלם ממון כפי הכרעת הבורר, ולתועלת העניין מן הראוי לעגן בתוך ההסכם שהתובעים יהיו הורי הילד, ובמדה ואי אפשר או עין רצונים בכך, אזי הנהלת המוסד.

40 ר' יהודה סילמן (ישורון חלק כב עמ' תקפ"ח): הנה נשאלתי בשעתו מארה"ב, בנידון דרישת השלטונות לדיווח במקרה של פגיעה מינית מצד מורה בתלמיכיו. האם מותר או מצווה לשתף פעולת ולדווח? והשבתי [ישורון ט"ו עמ' תרס"א] אז שיש לדון בזה מכמה מקורות: א) רודף [אלא שסיגתי שמה את הדברים שהיתר זה לא יועיל לבחור למעלה מבר מצוה או בת למעלה מ-12, והמבוגר עושה כן בהסכמת הבחור או הבת.] ב) לאפרושי מאיסורא, והבאתי מחלוקת הקצוה"ח ונתה"מ ר"ס ג והמשוובב שם, וכן דברי היש"ש ב"ק פ' המניח סי' ט ושו"ת חת"ס ח"מ סי' קעז, והעולה מדברי כולם דעכ"פ יחיד חשוב יכול להפריש בלא תעשה, ג) הך דש"ע ח"מ סי' ב שב"ד מכין ועונשין שלא מן הדין משום סייג, ובנידון כזה שהנסיון מראה שאדם כזה יכול לקלקל רבים הכל מודים שיכולים הב"ד לעשותו כך [ועיי"ש שנ"ז בין הטעמים, דלטעם של אפרושי אם יגיש התפטרות יש לשקול שא"צ, דעיקר ההזדמנות להזיק בטילה, ותלוי לפי חריפות העניין, ואילו לטעם של עשיית סייג יכולים אף בכה"ג. ד) הך דבבא מציעא (פג:) דדראב"ש הוה קא תפי גנבי ע"פ הורמנא דמלכא, והבאתי שם מחלוקת הראשונים אם הלכה כמותו או לא. ועיי"ש שצדדתי דאפשר דבנידון דילן שאין הורגים אלא מגינים על הציבור ע"י מאסר יודו כו"ע דשרי.

ועוד שם שפשוט שלכל הטעמים א"צ בכל זה לעדים כשרים, אלא ניתן לסמוך גם על פחות מזה, והבאתי לכם מכמה ראשונים. והטעם שאין זה עונש מדין ב"ד, אלא אם משום חוק המלכות (בחו"ל) או לאפרושי מאיסורא, וכן לפי הטעם שספק רודף שרי, פשוט דשרי בכה"ג דסגי בנהיה לנו ספק.

וכעת חוזרים ושואלים איזה ב"ד מוסמך לדון בעניינים אלו, ומה היא צורת הדיון הראוי, שיש אומרים דבעינן מושב ב"ד בנוכחות הצדדים, דלולא כך אי אפשר לעמוד על אמיתות הדברים.

וי"א להיפוך, ל"מ שא"צ מושב בית דין במעמד הצדדים, אלא אף זו, אפילו מעשה ב"ד או הוראת רב מוסמך א"צ, אלא העצה היעוצה לערב את הרשויות תיכף ומיד, הואיל ולהם בלבד אפשרות חוקית ומעשית לטפל בענין...

Responsa & comments of Gedolim

תשובה: א) הנה מצד אחד ז"ה שא"צ מושב ב"ד בנוכחות הצדדים, לפי האמור לעיל שסיבת ההיתר לדווח הוא או מדין ספק רודף, או מדין לאפרושי מאיסורא, או מדין הורמנא דמלכא, ולכל הטעמים לאו דין ב"ד הוא זה. ומה גם שיש לשקול הפסד נגד ריווח, כי בכל מקרה של ספק סביר, על הצד שהוא אמת, מדובר הרי בהצלת עשוק מיד עושקו, ומאידך על הצד שאינו אמת, בדרך כלל הרשויות יפטרו את החשוד לשלום.

ומצד שני, בוודאי שאי אפשר למסור דבר זה לכל אחד ואחד, כי לרוב אינשי אין את הידע תורני ו/או מקצועי לקבוע אפילו אם יש במקרה המדובר רגלים לדבר וחשש סביר, ומן ההכרח אם כן שיטפלו בעניינים אלו אך רק ב"ד קבוע, או עכ"פ רב מוסמך, ומתמחה היטב בהוראות הלכות אלו. וחזקה על הב"ד או הרב שיפעל תוך ייעוץ עם אנשי מקצוע לפי הצורך, וכבר כתוב בסדור מה"ר שבתי סופר (הקדמה פרטית סי' כט, ד"ה שבתי): "ידעתי כי מי שיודע מקצת החכמה ולא יגיע עד תכליתה חושב שיודע כל סתריה, ואינו מודה על האמת לעולם, ועל כיוצא בזה אמר בעל ספר מבחר הפנינים (שער החכמה סי' סב), אינו יודע והוא מראה בעצמו שיודע, סכל, הרחיקהו", – ומכלל לאו אתה שומע הן.

ויצויין עוד שלכל הנ"ל הוצרכנו בנוגע לשאלת חובת הדיווח, אבל בדרך כלל קודם לזה יש דין מקדמי האם לפטור את הנחשד ממשרתו, ולעניין זה ודאי א"צ ל"א מעשה ב"ד ועאו"כ כל כללי דיוון, ובנוכחות הצדדים דייקא, וכמ"ש בתשובתי הקודמת משו"ת שואל ומשיב שמספיק ספק שנייה כדי מחויבים להגל על הילדים, ויחושו החושדים לפשען עד שישוב בתשובה שלימה וסיגופים. והוכחד דבר זה מהא דהאי בישא לישנא עכ"פ מקצות אמת דאיתא במו"ק יח, ובגמ' נדא סא, האי לישנא בישא אף דלא מקבלים אותו למיחש ימהא מיבעי'...

⁴¹ **מנחת יצחק (ח: קמח):** בעניין אם מותר למסור לשלטונות את אלו המסכנים עוברי דרך ע"י אי זהירות בהנהגתם בכלי רכב.

הנני בזה ע"ד שאלתו היות שישנם כמה הנהגים בכלי רכב באופן המסכן את כל מי שנמצא לידם בדרכים, או בכלי רכב הסמוכים להם, ע"י כמה וכמה אופנים שחשבם במכתבו, האם מותר למסרם לשלטונות, אשר בדרך כלל מענישים אותם בקנסות כספיים, או בשלילת הרשיון - נהיגה לתקופה מסוימת או במאסרים, למען ישמעו וייראו וימנעו מדברים המסכנים את הציבור. ואף דעפ"י הלכה אסור למסור גופו או ממונו של ישראל לערכאות, אבל מי שמסכן הציבור אינו בכלל זה, וכמבואר ברמב"ם (חובל ומזיק ח:יא) ושו"ע (חו"מ שפח:יב) שכל המיצר הציבור ומצערן מותר למסרו ביד עכו"ם להכותו ולאסרו ולקנסו וכו', דבר ברור שכל אלו אלו שנוהגים באי זהירות ובצורה מופקרת לסכנת נפשות מכניסים את כל מי שנמצא סמוך להם, והלא נצטוינו להתרחק מהסכנה, וכל דבר המביאים לידי סכנה, ואולי ע"י נקיטת אמצעים ופעולות נגדם נרחיק את הסכנה ויתמעטו האסונות עכת"ד.

הנה ברמב"ם (ה:ט) איתא אסור למסור האדם ביד /עכו"ם/ בין בגופו בין בממונו ואפילו היה רשע ובעל עבירות, ואפילו הי' מיצר ומצערן וכו' ואח"כ (בהי"א) כתב, וכן כל המיצר לציבור ומצערן מותר למסרו ביד עכו"ם להכותו ולאסרו ולקנסו וכו' כנ"ל. והנה חפשתי בנושאי כלים להרמב"ם להראות המראה מקום להחילוק בין יחיד לציבור ולא מצאתי,...

ובנותי בספרים ומצאתי את שאהבה נפשי, הה"ה הגאוני עולם החת"ס והכת"ס ז"ל (בספריהם על מס' גיטין), שהעירו שם (גיטין ז.) על הרמב"ם דבמצער לציבור, דנושאי כליו לא הראו מקום לדין זה כנ"ל, וכתב החת"ס משום דמשמע מסוגיין (גיטין ז.) שם, דאי לאו דהוה לי' הצלה ע"י השכם והערב הי' מותר למוסרו, וזה שייך ביחיד

Child & Domestic Abuse

לעצמו, אבל בציבור קדירא דבי שותפי מי יערוב וישכם בעד כולם, ע"כ מותר למוסרו עיי"ש, ואחריו בא בנו הגאון הכת"ס בספרו (גיטין) שם, ומילא את דברי אביו הגאון ז"ל, וכתב וז"ל ואאמ"ו זצ"ל בחידושיו נתקשה מנ"ל להרמב"ם הא (דמצער לציבור מותר למוסרו) ונדחק, והנ"ל כשנדקדק בלשון קרא בעוד רשע לנגדי, תיבת בעוד קשה וכו', ונ"ל דהורה לנו בזה דלא שם לפי מחסום רק כ"ז שלא הרשיע רק נגדי, אבל כשיצער לרבים, וכך דרכם של רשעים וכו' מרעה אל רעה יצאו להרע ולצער רבים לא החשתי עוד וכו' עכ"ד. והרי שניהם נתכוונו לדבר אחד שמצאו מקור לדברי הרמב"ם הנ"ל בדברי הש"ס גיטין (ז.), ובזה יהי' ראי' לדברי הריב"ש כדלהלן. והנה ראיתי בתשו' הריב"ש (סי' רל"ט) שכתב באמצע התשובה, וז"ל גם מה שאמר נגד המוקדמין אין ראוי להקרא מסירה וכו' אבל מ"מ כל מקום מן הדברים הם נזק להקהל והוצאות ולבא במשפט עם זקני עמו ושריו, לא ימלט שמעון מהיות מיצר ומצער הצבור באמרו הדברים ההם, וראוי להענש על זה כפי מה שיראה בעיני הב"ד כמ"ש הרמב"ם (חובל ומזיק ח:ה), וכן כל המיצר לצבור ומצער אותם מותר למוסרו ביד השופטים להכותם ולאסרו ולקנסו אבל מפני צער יחיד אסור למוסרו ע"כ. וכן אם יראה בעיני הב"ד שהדור פרוץ וכו' ולפי צורך ירצו להעניש יותר מן הדין משום מגדר מילתא וכו' הרשות בידם וכו' עכ"ל. ...., והנה דינו של הריב"ש הנ"ל, הביא ג"כ הרמ"א (חו"מ שפח:ט), ...ודאתנן מן דברי הריב"ש דאף בדברים בעלמא של חירוף וגידוף שייך הא דהרמב"ם הנ"ל, דכל המצער לציבור וכו', והרי כל זה אתי שפיר מאד לפי"ד החת"ס והכת"ס דמקור מקומו טהור של דברי הרמב"ם הנ"ל, בדברי הש"ס דגיטין (ז.), דפירש"י העומדים עלי לחרף ולגדף, דש"מ תרתי, א' דביחיד משום צער של דברים אסור למוסרו, ב' דמשום צער הציבור מותר למוסרו אף לעכו"ם אף רק משום חירוף וגידוף כנ"ל, וא"כ מכ"ש לעונשו ע"י ישראל כדברי הריב"ש. ...., דהנה בסמ"ע שם (שפח:ל) כתב על דצער יחיד, וז"ל והיינו דוקא מפני צער דעלמא, אבל מסרו בממון, וכש"כ אם יסרו במכות ועונש הגוף מותר כמ"ש בס"א בהגה ועד"מ ס"ט וע' בטור (תכה:סב) עכ"ל, והנה כ"ז ש"מ ג"כ מהא דגיטין שם, כמ"ש בחת"ס שם, דאע"ג דממה שפירש"י שם העומדים עלי לחרף ולגדף, י"ל משום שהאמת כך הי' בגניבא, אבל מהא שפירש"י שם, אקרא בעוד רשע לנגדי, מריבנו ומקנטנו, מוכח דפשיטא לרש"י דאם הי' מצערו בממון וזיוף מותר למסרו, ואינו צריך להשכים ולהעריך כי הבא להורגך השכם להרגו, וכ"פ הרמב"ם (מחובל ומזיק ח:יא) וכו', אבל מפני צער יחיד אסור למוסרו וכו', משמע מצער בעלמא, אבל מפסידו מותר למוסרו שלא יפסידנו כמ"ש הרמ"א (חו"מ שפח:ט), וש"ך שם (שפח:נט וס') עכ"ל. ...והנה הטעם דהמוסר הוא משום שיש לו דין רודף כמ"ש ברמ"א (חו"מ שפח:יב), ובסמ"ע שם (חו"מ שפח:כט) עיי"ש, ודין רודף מבואר שם בש"ע /חו"מ/ (סי' תכ"א ס"א), דכל ישראל מצווין להצילו, כפי סדר ההצלה המבואר שם, וכתב שם הרמ"א דמי שמסכן רבים כגון שעוסק בזיופים דינו כרודף ומותר למוסרו למלכות, וכ"כ שם /חו"מ/ (סי' שפח:יב), דמי שעוסק בזיופים ויש לחוש שיזיק לרבים מתרין בו שלא יעשה ואם אינו משגיח יכולין למסרו וכו'..., ונבוא לנד"ד, דפשיטא דבנוסע במהירות מופרזת אשר לא יוכל לעצור את הרכב ברגע שיצטרך לעצור מבלי לגרום אסון, שהזכיר כ"מ במכתבו, דדינו כרודף, דהרי אף בהרבה פחות מזה...., ואם אחרי ההתראה והאזהרה הוא ממשיך כרצונו, מותר למוסרו לשלטונות, - וכמו כן פשיטא במה שנזכר עוד במכתבו, כגון באינו עוצר הרכב בשעה שמסומן עבורו, שיוכלו הולכי רגל לעבור הכביש, וכן ברכב הבא ממכוון אחר לנסוע, או שעוקף רכב אחר בצורה המסכנת עבורו, - או שנוהג רכב מבלי שעבר את הבחינה שיודע לנהוג ברכב ולשלוט עליו בעת הצורך - דכל אלו בכלל רודף המסכן עצמם ואחרים, ואף אם אין כוונתו לסכן הוי בכלל רודף כנ"ל. וגם בכלל, אם מעמיד את רכבו בצורה המסכנת את הולכי רגל, או על המדרכה שמאלץ את הולכי הרגל לרדת על פני הכביש שזה מקום מיועד עבור נסיעת כלי רכב ומסוכן עבור הולכי רגל וכיב"ז שהזכיר במכתבו, כל אלה יש להם דין כמו חופר ברה"ר...אמנם כמבואר בש"ע בכל אלו הדינים בין ברודף /חו"מ/ (בסי' תכ"ה) ובין במוסר /חו"מ/ (סי' שפ"ח סעי' י') ובין בעוסק בזיופים (סעי' י"ב) ובשאר מקומות,

Responsa & comments of Gedolim

דקודם שימסור אותו לערכאות צריכים התראה, כן בנד"ד אין לעשות מעשה בלא התראת ב"ד, ובכן יש להעסקנים במצוה זו של הצלת נפשות לבוא לפני ב"ד ולהציע הצעתם לפניהם, ויה"ר שחפץ ד' בידכם יצליח וכאשר יצא דבר הב"ד יסכימו ג"כ מן השמים לטובת ותקנת הרבים.

[42] **נשמת אברהם (ד:רח סי' שפח:א - אסור למסור ע' ר"ז-רי"א):**. ואם מדובר על מעשה אונס בבית ספר של קטנים, כשהמורה מבצע מעשה מגונה בנערים או בנערות הקטנות. בראה שבמקרה של נערים ששוב מדובר על מעשה שיש בה משום מיתת בית דין, ויש לו דין של רודף שיהיה מותר למוסרו וכבשני המקרים הקודמים. אך גם במקרה שמדובר על מעשה מגונה בנערות, נראה שיהיה מותר לרופא שמגלה את הדבר, להודיע עליו למנהל בית הספר ואם בכל זאת לא נעשה דבר, יהיה מותר לו להודיע למשטרה, אפילו בחוץ לארץ, כי מכיון שמדובר על מי שמיצר לרבים, אין כאן איסור של מסירה [חו"מ שפח:יב לפי גירסת הש"ך והגר"א.] ואדרבה חייבים לעשות זאת כדי שאותו מורה לא ימשיך בדרכו הרעה לא בבית ספר זה ולא בבית ספר אחר. ובדרור שבכל המקרים אין לרופא לנקוט שום פעולה בלי שהוא משוכנע שהדבר נכון ולפני שהוא מתייעץ עם מורה הוראה מובהק, כי בנפשו הוא. ואמר לי הגר"ש אלישיב שליט"א שאין הבדל בין נערים ונערות כי מדובר בכל אופן על פגיעה נפשית חמורה וכן סכנה לרבים. ... קצרתי מתוך תשובת הרשב"א הנזכרת, עכ"ל של הב"י. ועל זה אמר לי הגאון שליט"א שכל שכן הוא בשאלתנו כשמדובר על דבר שהוא הרבה יותר חמור מגניבה, שודאי מותר קודם למסור כל הדבר למנהל בית הספר ואם בכל זאת לא נעשה שום דבר בענין, גם למשטרה ואפילו בחוץ לארץ, עכ"ד. .

[43] **נשמת אברהם (ד:רח סי' שפח:א - אסור למסור ע' ר"ז-רי"א):**. ילד או תינוק שהובא לבית חולים עם תסמונת "הילד המוכה", דהיינו עם שברים מרובים בגולגולת או בגפיים , או עם דימומים באברים הפנימיים עקב מכות או בעיטות קשות, או עם כוויית קשות מאש, חשמל או מים רותחים וכו'. שנעשתה באכזריות ובמזיד ע"י אחד או שני הוריו. אסור אחרי הטיפול המושלם, להחזירו אותו לביתו כי אז ימשיכו להכות בו עד המות. בגלל סכנת הנפשות הממשית, על הרופא להודיע לבית שמשפט ואז ע"י צו בית המשפט מעבירים את התינוק למשפחה אומנת או למוסד. נראה שאין בזה שאלה של מוסר מכיון שמדובר בסכנת נפשות של ממש ולהורים דין של רודף, ויתכן שמותר גם אם מעבירים את התינוק, בלית ברירה, למשפחה או למוסד לא דתי. אך כמובן יצטרך בית דין לעשות הכל שביכולתו לדאוג לזה שהילד יועבר למשפחה או למוסד שומר תורה ומצוות. ובמיוחד בחוץ לארץ על הבית דין לדאוג שלא יועבר הילד למשפחה או מוסד של עכו"ם. והסכים אתי הגרש"ז אויערבאך שליט"א.

ואמר לי הגר"ש אלישיב שליט"א שמותר לרופא להודיע לשלטונות אפילו כשקיים ספק [בחוץ לארץ] שילד יישלח למשפחה או מוסד של גויים אך אחרי כך עליו לעשות בכל יכולתו לראות לזה שהילד יימסר למשפחה או מוסד יהודיים.

[44] **נשמת אברהם (ד:רח סי' שפח:א - אסור למסור ע' ר"ז-רי"א):**. ילד או תינוק שהובא לבית חולים עם תסמונת "הילד המוכה", דהיינו עם שברים מרובים בגולגולת או בגפיים , או עם דימומים באברים הפנימיים עקב מכות או בעיטות קשות, או עם כוויית קשות מאש, חשמל או מים רותחים וכו'. שנעשתה באכזריות ובמזיד ע"י אחד או שני הוריו. אסור אחרי הטיפול המושלם, להחזירו אותו לביתו כי אז ימשיכו להכות בו עד המות. בגלל סכנת הנפשות הממשית, על הרופא להודיע לבית שמשפט ואז ע"י צו בית המשפט מעבירים את התינוק למשפחה אומנת או למוסד. נראה שאין בזה שאלה של מוסר מכיון שמדובר בסכנת נפשות של ממש ולהורים דין של רודף, ויתכן שמותר גם אם מעבירים את התינוק, בלית

Child & Domestic Abuse

ברירה, למשפחה או למוסד לא דתי. אך כמובן יצטרך בית דין לעשות הכל שביכולתו לדאוג לזה שהילד לא יועבר למשפחה או למוסד שומר תורה ומצוות. ובמיוחד בחוץ לארץ על הבית דין לדאוג שלא יועבר הילד למשפחה או מוסד של עכו"ם. והסכים אתי הגרש"ז אויערבאך שליט"א.

ואמר לי הגר"ש אלישיב שליט"א שמותר לרופא להודיע לשלטונות אפילו כשקיים ספק [בחוץ לארץ] שילד יישלח למשפחה או מוסד של גויים אך אחרי כך עליו לעשות בכל יכולתו לראת לזה שהילד יימסר למשפחה או מוסד יהודיים.

[45] הגרי"ש אלישיב (קובץ תשובות ג:רלא):

... תוכן השאלה אחד יודע שמישהו מתעלל בילד או בילדה בעניני מין, ובאופן שאין בידינו לעצור בעדו שלא ימשיך במעשיו הרעים, האם מותר להודיע על כך לפקיד הממשלה?

והנה ז"ל הרשב"א בתשובה (ג:שצג): "רואה אני שאם העדים נאמנים אצל הברורים רשאים הן לקנוס קנס ממון או עונש הגוף הכל לפי מה שיראה להם וזה מקיים העולם שאם אתם מעמידין הכל על הדינים הקצובים בתורה ושלא לענוש אלא כמו שענשה התורה - נמצא העולם חרב - ונמצאו פורצין גדרו של עולם נמצא העולם שמם, וכבר קנסו קנסות במכה את חבירו וכו' בכל מקום ומקום דנין לגדור את הדור וכן עושין בכל דור ודור ובכל מקום ומקום שרואין שהשעה צריכה לכן - והנה אמרו דרב הונא שהיה מבבל קץ ידא - ולפיכך ברורים אלו שעשו זה אם ראו צורך השעה לתיקון המדינה - כדין עשר, - וכ"כ בדאיכא הורמנא דמלכא וכענין שעשן ר' אלעזר בר"ש בר"פ הפועלים" [בבא מציעא פג.].

מתוך דברי הרשב"א שמעינן דבדבר שיש בה משום תיקון העולם יש כח לחכמי ישראל בכל דור ודור לגדור גדר ולעמוד בפרץ גם במקום שאין לנו צירוף של הורמנא דמלכא וממ"ש הריטב"א בחי' לבבא מציעא[פד:] משמע לכאורה דכחו של הורמנא דמלכא הוא וז"ל שאני הכא דשליחא יאמר להן תפסוהו, והא דדאין בלא עדים והתראה, ושלא בזמן סנהדרין, שאני הכא דשליחא דמלכא הוא ומדיני המלכות להרוג בלא עדים והתראה כמו"ש בדוד שהרג גר עמלקי ושלוחו של מלך כמותו -", אך כפי האמור בדבר שיש בו משום תיקון העולם א"צ בקבלת הורמנא דמלכא.

אכן כ"ז להתיר להודיע לממשלה הוא באופן שהדבר ברור שאכן ידו במעל, ובזה יש משום תיקון העולם אך באופן שאין אפי' רגלים לדבר, אלא איזה דמיון אם נתיר הדבר לא רק שאין בזה משום תיקון העולם אלא הרס העולם יש כאן ויתכן שבגלל איזה מרירות של תלמיד כלפי המורה מעליל על המורה או בגלל איזה דמיון שוא מכניסים אדם למצב שטוב מותו מחייו. - על לא עול בכפו, ואין אני רואה שום היתר בדבר.

[46] ר' יוסף שלום אלישיב (דברי סיני - ירושלים תש"ס ע' מה-מו): שאלה: ממשרד המועצה הדתית במקומנו נגנב מהקופה פעמים אחסות כסף מזומן. לפי כל הסימנים יד אחד מהעובדים בזה, אולם אין בידינו האמצעים בישביאו לידי הודאתו. נשאלת השאלה אם מותר לפנות למשטרה אשר אחרי חקירתה, אם תצליח, תביא את החשוד למשפט החיתוני. המסקנות עלולות להיות חמרורת, כי עלול שהחשוד הוא בעל מפשחה גדולה. נוסף לכך אם זה מישהו שקשור עם עבודת הקודש, עלול להיות חלילה גם חילול ה', ר"ל. מאדך גיסא, יתכן שכספי ציבור נעלמים ומי יודע מה עוד. תשובה: עיין בשו"ת פנים מאירות ח"ב סי' קנה, מ"ש בנידונו בא' שמצא תיבה פרוצה ונגנב מתוכה הון רב, ויש לו אומדנות המוכיחות שאחד ממשרתיו עשה את המעשה הזה, אי שרי לי' למוסרו לערכאות, ע"פ אומדן יעצו שיודע באמת. והביא שם מעשה רב מהבאון העשל והש"ך, עי"ש. אלא שבסוף הוא מסיק "וחכך אני מאוד שלא למוסרו לערכאותיהם, וכבר אמרו רז"ל כתוא

Responsa & comments of Gedolim

מכמר, יש לחוש שאם יודה, ידונו אותו למיתה." ומכאן דזה לא שייך בזמננו. הרי מן הדין ראשים לפנות למשטרה, אולם לפי"ד כת"ר עלול להיות חילול השם. ואין בידי להביע דעה ע"ז, הואיל ואיני יודע את העניו, והדבר נתון אפוא לשיקול דעת כת"ר.

[47] **ר' אלישיב (ישורון טו' תרמב)**: ע"ד השאלה במקרה וההורים מתעוללים בילדיהם [מכות לילד] והחוק מחייב למסור הדבר לפקיד הממשלה והממשלה עלולה להוציא הילד מבית ההורים ולהשיבם בבתים אחרים אף בבית של נכרי, עד שיתברר הדבר ע"י ראשים למסור הדבר לממשלה באופן שאכן אמת נכון הדבר. תשובה: הדבר תלוי בכמה גרומים, אם הילד נצמא בבית שומרי תו"מ ומתחין בבתיהם הרי ע"י מסירת הילד לבית נכרי ואף לבית חילוני ה"ז בגדר מסירה זרע ישראל למולך כי אין ספק שזה יפגע הילד גם אם זה לזמן קצר וזה ישפיע על חינוכו של הילד בעתיד [מדובר במקרה שאין בהתכוללות ההורים שמום פקו"נ] יש גם לשקול בגדר של ההתעוללות, שבהשקפה שלהם היא אחרת לגמרי משלנו. ובכן איפוא על כל מקרה ומקרה צריך שיקול דעת והכרעה ע"י ת"ח גדולים בתורה ויר"ש.

[48] **שולחן ערוך (חושן משפט ב:א)**: כל בית דין, אפילו אינם סמוכים בא"י, אם רואים שהעם פרוצים בעבירות (ושהוא צורך שעה) (טור), היו דנין בין מיתה בין ממון, בין בכל דיני עונש, ואפילו אין בדבר עדות גמורה. ואם הוא אלם, חובטים אותו על ידי עובדי כוכבים. (ויש להם כח להפקיר ממונו ולאבדו כפי מה שרואים לגדור פרצת הדור) (טור בשם הרמב"ם בפרק כ"ד מסנהדרין). וכל מעשיהם יהיו לשם שמים; ודוקא גדול הדור, או טובי העיר שהמחום ב"ד עליהם. הגה: וכן נהגין בכל מקום שטובי העיר בעירן כב"ד הגדול, מכין ועונשין, והפקרן הפקר כפי המנהג; אעפ"י שיש חולקין וס"ל דאין כח ביד טובי העיר באלה, רק להכריח הצבור במה שהיה מנהג מקדם או שקבלו עליהם מדעת כולם, אבל אין רשאים לשנות דבר במדי דאיכא רווחא להאי ופסידא להאי, או להפקיע ממון שלא מדעת כולם (מרדכי פ' הגוזל בתרא), מכל מקום הולכין אחר מנהג העיר; וכל שכן אם קבלום עליהם לכל דבר, כן נ"ל (ועיין בי"ד סימן רכ"ח דיני תקנות וחרמי צבור). כתבו האחרונים בתשובותיהם דמי שנתחייב מלקות, יתן ארבעים זהובים במקום מלקות (מהרי"ו סימן קמ"ז ומהר"ם מריזבורק); ולאו דינא קאמר, אלא שהם פסקו כך לפי שעה, אבל ביד הב"ד להלקותו או ליטול ממון כפי ראות עיניהם, לפי העניו, למגדר מלתא (וע"ל ריש סימן תכ"ה בהג"ה).

[49] **שולחן ערוך (חושן משפט ד:א)**: יכול אדם לעשות דין לעצמו; אם רואה שלו ביד אחר שגזלו, יכול לקחתו מידו; ואם האחר עומד כנגדו, יכול להכותו עד שיניחנו, (אם לא יוכל להציל בעניו אחר) (טור), אפילו הוא דבר שאין בו הפסד אם ימתין עד שיעמידנו בדין, והוא שיוכל לברר ששלו הוא נוטל בדין; מ"מ אין לו רשות למשכנו בחובו...

[50] **שולחן ערוך (חושן משפט כו:ב)**: היתה יד עובדי כוכבים תקיפה, ובעל דינו אלם, ואינו יכול להציל ממנו בדייני ישראל, יתבענו לדייני ישראל תחלה; אם לא רצה לבא, נוטל רשות מבית דין ומציל בדייני עובד כוכבים מיד בעל דינו. הגה: ויש רשות לבית דין לילך לבית דין של עובדי כוכבים ולהעיד שזה חייב לזה (בה"ת בשם ר' שרירא). וכל זה דווקא כשאינו רוצה לציית דין, אבל בלאו הכי אסור לבית דין להרשות לדון לפני עובדי כוכבים (מהרי"ק שורש א').

[51] **שולחן ערוך (חושן משפט לה:יד)**: אשה, פסולה... הגה: וכל אלו הפסולים, פסולים אפילו במקום דלא שכיחא אנשים כשרים להעיד (הרשב"א בתשובה והרמב"ם בפ"ח נזקי ממון וכ"כ הב"י), וכל זה מדינא, אבל י"א דתקנת קדמונים הוא במקום שאין אנשים רגילים להיות, כגון בב"ה של נשים או בשאר דבר אקראי שאשה רגילה ולא אנשים, כגון לומר שבגדים אלו לבשה אשה פלונית והן שלה, ואין רגילים אנשים לדקדק בזה, נשים נאמנות (ת"ה סי' שנ"ג ואגודה פ' י'

Child & Domestic Abuse

יוחסין). ולכן יש מי שכתב דאפילו אשה יחידה, או קרוב או קטן, נאמנים בענין הכאה ובזיון ת"ח או שאר קטטות ומסירות, לפי שאין דרך להזמין עדים כשרים לזה, ואין פנאי להזמין (מהרי"ק שורש קע"ט ומהר"ם מריזבורג וכלבו סי' קט"ז). והוא שהתובע טוען ברי (מהרי"ק שורש כ"ג /צ"ג/) (וע"ל סכ"ח סט"ו בהג"ה).

[52] **שולחן ערוך (חושן משפט שפח:יב)**: כל המוסר הצבור ומצערן, מותר למסרו ביד עובדי כוכבים אנסים להכותו ולאסרו ולקנסו; אבל מפני צער יחיד אסור למסרו. הגה: (וע"ל סי' תכ"ה ס"א). מי שעוסק בזיופים וכדומה, ויש לחוש שיזיק רבים, מתרין בו שלא יעשה, ואם אינו משגיח, יכולין למסרו ולומר שאין אחר מתעסק בו אלא זה לבד. מי שרוצה לברוח ולא לשלם לעובדי כוכבים מה שחייב, ואחר גילה הדבר, אין לו דין מוסר, שהרי לא הפסידו רק שהוצרך לשלם מה שחייב, מכל מקום ברעה עשה כמשיב אבידה לעובד כוכבים; ואם גרם לו היזק, חייב לשלם לו מה שגרם לו (מהר"ם מרוזבורג).

[53] **שולחן ערוך (חושן משפט שפח:ט)**: אסור למסור לישראל ביד עובדי כוכבים אנסים; בין בגופו בין בממונו, ואפילו היה רשע ובעל עבירות; ואפילו היה מיצר לו ומצערו. הגה: ודוקא בדברים בעלמא; אבל אם מסרו, מותר למסרו, דהרי יכול להרגו בדין במקום שיש חשש שיחזור וימסרנו לאנסים (הרא"ש כלל י"ז סי' א', וב' ותשו' רשב"א סי' קפ"א); או אם אי אפשר להציל עצמו בדרך אחר; אבל אם אפשר להציל עצמו בדרך אחר; הוי כשנים שמסרו זה את זה, וכל מי שהפסיד חבירו יותר חייב לשלם בנזק שלם המותר לו (מרדכי פ' הנ"ל ותשובת מיימוני לס' נזיקין סימן ט"ו). וכל המוסר ישראל ביד עובד כוכבים, בין בגופו בין בממונו, אין לו חלק לעולם הבא.

[54] **שולחן ערוך (חושן משפט תכא:יג)**: ...וכן הדין באדם הרואה אחד מישראל מכה חבירו, ואינו יכול להצילו אם לא שיכה את המכה, יכול להכותו, כדי לאפרושי מאיסורא. הגה: וכן מי שהוא תחת רשותו, ורואה בו שהוא עושה דבר עבירה, רשאי להכותו וליסרו כדי להפרישו מאיסור, ואין צריך להביאו לבית דין (ת"ה סי' י"ח /רי"ח/).

[55] **נשמת אברהם (ד:רח סי' שפח:א - אסור למסור ע' ר"ז-רי"א)**: וכתב לי הגרא"י וולדינברג שליט"א: דאם קיימת ממש חשש מבוסס שהוריו ישובו קרוב לודאי להכותו שוב, ועוד יותר מזה, ועד למות, במקרה כזה, שמכיון שהרופא רק מוסר על המצב למשטרה ובבקשה לראות להציל את התינוק מידי הורוי, אזי חייב לעשות זאת כדי להציל נפש אחת מישראל ממות, ומה שיעשה אחר מכן המשרד הממשלתי כדי להצילו הרי הרופא בזה רק בחינה של גורם בלבד, ואין לפני עור ממש כי הרי לא בטוח כי הרי אחוז במאה שיעבירו אותו דוקא למוסד של עכו"ם, או לא דתי, ונוסף לזה גם התינוק עד שיגדל איננו עובר עי"כ שום עבירה, וכשיגדל הרי יתכן גם שיחזירוהו למקום שיוכל לשמור על יהדותו, עכ"ל.

[56] **נשמת אברהם (ד:רח סי' שפח:א - אסור למסור ע' ר"ז-רי"א)**: ואם מדובר על מעשה אונס, למשל, כשהאב אונס את בתו הקטנה פעמים חוזרות, הרי גם כאן יש לאב דין של רודף ונראה שהדין יהיה כפי שבמקרה דלעיל. וכתב לי הגרש"ז אויערבאך שליט"א: כאשר יקום איש על רעהו ורצחו נפש כן הדבר הזה והוא ממש רודף אחר עריות, עכ"ל. וכן כתב לי הגרא"י וולדינברג שליט"א: לדעתי הדין בזה כפי שהעליתי בשאלה הקודמת, כי הרי דין רודף אחר הערוה כדין רודף אחר תבירו להרגו, והבא על בתו הרי הוא מחייבי כריתות, והגם שהיא קטנה אבל הוא חייב על כך, ומן החובה להפרישו מזה... וממשיך הגרא"י וולדינברג שליט"א וכותב: על המקרים האמורים בא בכבודו בשאלה נוספת בנוגע לדין מוסר וכו'. תשובה: אפילו אילו לא היתה ערוה עליו שחייבים על זה כרת, גם כן היה מותר למוסרו, הן כדי להציל אותה מפגיעתו וגם לרבות כדי להציל אותו מרשעתו זה, ומה שכבר' מצטט ממה שפסק בחו"מ סי' שפח סע' ט שאסור למסור בחו"מ אפילו הוא רשע ובעל עבירות, אין לו ענין לעל כגון נידוננו, דבשם אין המדובר שבא הדבר כדי להציל אותו מרשעתו, אלא שרוצים למסור אותו

Responsa & comments of Gedolim

נשביל דבר אחר ורוצים לנהוג בו זלזול בגלל זה שבין כך הוא רשע ובעל עבירות, ומשא"כ בכגון נידוננו שרוצים ע"י להציל אותו מלהוציא לפועל זממת רשעתו, ילכן שפיר מותר. אמרנו שמותר זה גם בכדי להציל אותה מפגיעתו בה, כי אין זה דומה גם למה שנפסק בשו"ע שם שאסור אפילו היה מצר לו ומצערו, דבכאן הרי פוגע ע"כ בגופה ובנפשה, ועיין בשו"ע שם בס"ע ז שנפסק ברמ"א די"א דאדם המוכה מהבירו יכול לילך לקבל בפני עכו"ם דגורם למכה היזק גדול, והש"ך בס"ק מה כותב בכעין החילוק הנ"ל דשאני היכא שמוסר כדי שלא יוסיף להכות דמותר ע"ש, ומקרה כזה שלפנינו הוא יותר גרוע מהכאה וא"כ יכולים למוסרו הן מפני שזה דומה למכה, והן כדי שלא יוסיף עשות זאת, ובית דין אביהם של קטנים, עכ"ל.

[57] **נשמת אברהם (ד:רח סי' שפח:א - אסור למסור ע' ר"ז-רי"א):.** ואם מדובר על מעשה אונס בבית ספר של קטנים, כשהמורה מבצע מעשה מגונה בנערים או בנערות הקטנות. בראה שבמקרה של נערים ששוב מדובר על מעשה שיש בה משום מיתת בית דין, ויש לו דין של רודף שיהיה מותר למוסרו וכבשני המקרים הקודמים. אך גם במקרה שמדובר על מעשה מגונה בנערות, נראה שיהיה מותר לרופא שמגלה את הדבר, להודיע עליו למנהל בית הספר ואם בכל זאת לא נעשה דבר, יהיה מותר לו להודיע למשטרה, אפילו בחוץ לארץ, כי מכיון שמדובר על מי שמיצר לרבים, אין כאן איסור של מסירה [חו"מ שפח:יב לפי גירסת הש"ך והגר"א]. ואדרבה חייבים לעשות זאת כדי שאותו מורה לא ימשיך בדרכו הרעה לא בבית ספר זה ולא בבית ספר אחר. וברור שבכל המקרים אין לרופא לנקוט שום פעולה בלי שהוא קודם כל משוכנע שהדבר נכון ולפני שהוא מתייעץ עם מורה הוראה מובהק, כי בנפשו הוא. ...וכתב לי הגרא"י וולדינברג שליט"א: ומהאמור לעיל. הדבר פשוט כבר ממילא, שגם בשאלה ג' שמפרט כבו' במכתבו, על מקרים ידועים של התעללות מינית של מורה בבית ספר לילדים, שמותר למוסרו, ועוד בקל והומר, מכיון שמדובר גם באדם שמיצר את הרבים ומצערן, כנפסק בחו"מ שם סע' יב וכפי שמציין שפיר כבו' במכתבו.

[58] **נשמת אברהם (ד:רח סי' שפח:א - אסור למסור ע' ר"ז-רי"א):.** ילד או תינוק שהובא לבית חולים עם תסמונת "הילד המוכה", דהיינו עם שברים מרובים בגולגולת או בגפיים, או עם דימומים באברים הפנימיים עקב מכות או בעיטות קשות, או עם כוויות קשות מאש, חשמל או מים רותחים וכו'. שנעשה באכזריות ובמזיד ע"י אחד או שני הוריו. אסור אחרי הטיפול המושלמים, להחזיר אותו לביתו כי אז ימשיכו להכות בו עד המוות. בגלל סכנת הנפשות הממשית, על הרופא להודיע לבית המשפט ואז ע"י צו בית המשפט מעבירים את התינוק למשפחה אומנת או למוסד. נראה שאין בזה שאלה של מוסר מכיון שמדובר בסכנת נפשות של ממש והלורים דין של רודף, ויתכן שמותר גם אם מעבירים את התינוק, בלית ברירה, למשפחה או למוסד לא דתי. אך כמובן יצטרך בית דין לעשות הכל שביכולתו לדאוג לזה שהילד יועבר למשפחה או למוסד שומר תורה ומצוות. ובמיוחד בחוץ לארץ שיש דין לדאוג על הבית לא יועבר הילד למשפחה או מוסד של עכו"ם. והסכים אתי הגרש"ז אויערבאך שליט"א.

ואמר לי הגר"ש אלישיב שליט"א שמותר לרופא להודיע לשלטונות אפילו כשקיים ספק [בחוץ לארץ] שילד יישלח למשפחה או מוסד של גויים אך אחרי כך עליו לעשות בכל יכולתו לראות לזה שהילד יימסר למשפחה או מוסד יהודיים.

וכתב לי הגרא"י וולדינברג שליט"א: דאם קיימת ממש חשש מבוסס שהוריו ישובו לודאי להכותו שוב, ועוד יותר מזה, ועד למות, במקרה כזה, שמכיון שהרופא רק מוסר על המצב למשטרה ובבקשה לראות להציל את התינוק מידי הוריו, אזי חייב לעשות זאת כדי להציל נפש אחת מישראל ממות, ומה שיעשה אחר מיכן המשרד הממשלתי כדי להצילו הרי

145

Child & Domestic Abuse

הרופא בזה רק בבחינה של גורם בלבד, ואין לפני עור ממש כי הרי לא בטוח במאה אחוז שיעבירו אותו דוקא למוסד של עכו"ם, או לא דתי, ונוסף לזה גם התינוק איננו עובר ע"כ שום עבירה, וכשיגדל הרי יתכן גם שיחזירוהו למקום שיוכל לשמור על יהדותו, עכ"ל.

[59] **ציץ אליעזר (חלק טו סימן יג:א): א)** שאלתו הראשונה היא במקרה והרופא מוצא אצל חולה ליקוי בראייה, ... אשר לדעת הרופא עלול לגרום - בתנאים מסויימים - לתאונה ... והחולה אינו רוצה להפסיק לנהוג ברכב או לשנות את מקום עבודתו, האם חייב הרופא לשמור את סוד המחלה, או שמחויב להודיע לשלטונות המתאימים (משרד התחבורה, צבא, מעביד וכו') על מגבלות החולה, הגם שעי"כ יגרום אולי נזק כלכלי או חברתי לחולה, ומה אם החולה מבקש לשמור בסוד את קיום המחלה ומבטיח להמנע מנהיגה וכו', אבל הרופא אינו משוכנע שאמנם כך יעשה החולה? וזאת תשובתו על זה.

בודאי מחויב הרופא להודיע לשלטונות המתאימים ולמעבידו של החולה על מגבלותיו, ואפילו אם החולה מבקש לשמור את קיום המחלה ומבטיח להמנע מנהיגה וכו', כל עוד שהרופא איננו משוכנע שאמנם כך יעשה, מחויב ג"כ להודיע כנד', ולא מיבעיא אם מזמינים אותו להעיד על כך שמחויב ללכת ולהעיד, ולא חלה על כגון דא שבועת - הרופאים הכללית לשמור סודיות רפואית וגם לא הבטחה ושבועה פרטית, כי הוה ליה כנשבע לבטל את המצוה דלא חלה השבועה, וגם מסתבר שהשבועה הכללית של הרופאים לא היתה בכלל על כגון דא, שלא לגלות דבר שבהמנעותו מזאת תהיה עבירה בידו, וכפי שביארתי מכל זה וביתר אריכות בספרי שו"ת ציץ אליעזר ח"ג סי' פ"א אותיות ב' ג' יעו"ש, אלא אפילו אם לא מזמינים אותו להעיד מחויב הוא גם כן מעצמו להודיע על הדבר לשלטונות המתאימים, בהיות דאחרת יוכל הדבר להגיע ולגרום לפעמים לידי סיכון חיי אנשים אחרים, ולא עוד, אלא אם הרופא מונע את עצמו מלהודיע כנד' הרי הוא עובר על הלאו של לא תעמוד על דם רעך, ולכן אין לו להתחשב בכגון זה מה שעי"כ יגרום אולי נזק כלכלי או חברתי לחולה, כי אין לך דבר העומד בפני פקוח נפש.

אוסיף בזה מה שמצאתי בספר פתחי תשובה על או"ח (בעהמח"ס תוספת ירושלים ואשי ישראל ועוד) סי' קנ"ו שכותב וז"ל: וראיתי להזכיר פה ע"ד אשר כל הספרי מוסר הרעישו את העולם על עון לשון הרע, ואנכי מרעיש העולם להיפוך עון גדול מזה וגם הוא מצוי יותר, והוא מניעת עצמו מלדבר במקום הנצרך להציל העשוק מיד עושקו, ... עכ"ל, והדברים מאד מאלפים ומחזקים ביתר שאת וביתר עז דברינו האמורים בזה, ובלבד שכל הכוונה תהא לא להזיק לו כי אם לטובת השני ולטובת הכלל להצילם ולשמרם דאזי מקיים עוד ע"כ מצוה רבה שאין ערוך לה.

וכך מצאתי עוד בסבר שו"ת חלקת יעקב (ג:קלו) שנשאל למעשה אודות בחור אחד שיש לו רח"ל מחלת הסרטן ל"ע, ולהחולה עצמו ולמשפחתו לא נודע כלל מזה, והוא נתארס לנערה לינשא עמה אם הרופא מחויב לגלות זאת לכלה בהיות ולדעת הרופאים לא יחיה יותר משנה או שנתיים, וכמובן שבהודיעו זאת לכלה לא תנשא עמו, והשיב שמחויב הרופא לגלות זאת להכלה, כשהנימוק ההלכתי הראשי שלו בזה הוא מפני דאחרת הוא יעבור על הלאו של לא תעמוד על דם רעך, ובהסתמכו על הנפסק ברמב"ם (מרוצח יד ובחו"מ סי' תכ"ו), דהרואה את חבירו טובע בים וכו' או חיה רעה באה עליו או ששמע עכו"ם או מומרים מחשבים עליו רעה או טומנים לו פח, ולא גילה אוזן חבירו, וכיוצא בדברים אלו עובר על לא תעמוד על דם רעך עיי"ש, ומינה במכל שכן על כגון נידננו שהדבר יכול להגיע עד כדי גרימה לסיכונם הממשי של חיי אחרים, שבודאי ובודאי אם לא יגלה הרופא זאת למקומות המתאימים מבעוד מועד הוא יעבור בהמנעותו על הלאו של לא

146

Responsa & comments of Gedolim

תעמוד על דם רעך, ולכן בודאי ובודאי כי מותר לו לרופא, וגם מחויב בכך להודיע לשלטונות המתאימים על מגבלות החולה..

ציץ אליעזר (יט:נב): שאלה. א) ילד המוכה.[60] לדאבוני אין הדבר נדיר שמביאים תינוק או ילד לביה"ח כשהוא כולו פצוע קשה עם שברים בגולגולת ובגפיים, דימומים באברים פנימיים, ממכות או כוויות קשות (ממים רותחים או מסגריות וכדומה) עד מצב של ממש פקוח נפש, כשכל החבלות האלו נעשו במזיד ע"י אחד או שני הורי, וכפי שכתבתי כבר בחחו"מ של ספרי (סימן תכ"ד סק"ב עמוד רי"ט) כשמתלוננים במשטרה, אז אחרי שהתינוק טופל ומשתחרר מביה"ח מעבירים אותו ע"י צו בית המשפט למשפחה אומנת או למוסד כדי להציל אותו מהוריו, כי כבר היו מקרים לא מועטים שכשהחזירו את התינוק לביתו, מוכה אח"כ למוות, שאלתי היא מה יהיה הדין כשהרופא יודע שהסיכויים הם טובים שיעבירו את התינוק לבית או למוסד לא דתי, או אפילו בחו"ל לבית או מוסד של עכו"ם, האם עדיין עליו להתלונן למשטרה, או לא?

ב) במקרה שהאבא בא על בתו הקטנה פעמים חוזרות ואין כאן חשש של פיקו"נ מה הדין כאן לגבי הספיקות שהשאלתי לעיל?

ג) יהיה מותר למסור אותו (חו"מ סימן שפ"ח סעי' י"ב לפי גירסת הש"ך והגר"א) וכן בשאלה (א) שמדובר על פיקו"נ ויש לו דין של רודף, אך מה יהא הדין בשאלה (ב) הלא כותב השו"ע (שם סעי' ט) שאסור "ואפילו הוא רשע ובעל עבירות ואפילו היה מצר לו ומצערו" האם מדובר גם על מקרה כזה כשיש נזק של ממש גם פיזית וודאי נפשית?

ברור לי שבכל מקרה ומקרה חייב הרופא להתייעץ קודם כל עם מורה הוראה מובהק שישקול בכל מקרה לגופו של דבר. אך אבקש מאד חוות דעתו של כ"ת בנושא כואב זה. [...]

תשובה. א) בקשר לשאלתו הראשונה, לענ"ד נראה בכזאת. דאם קיים ממש חשש מבוסס שהורי הילד ישובו קרוב לודאי להכותו שוב במכות אכזריות כאלה, ועד יותר מזה עד למות, במקרה כזה, מכיון שהרופא רק מוסר על המצב למשטרה עם בקשה לראות להציל את הילד מידי הוריו, אזי חייב הרופא לעשות זאת כדי להציל נפש אחת מישראל מרדת שחת, ומה שיעשה לאחר מיכן המשרד הממשלתי כדי להצילו הרי הרופא בזה רק מציל בבחינה של גורם בלבד, ואין לפני עור ממש כי הרי לא בטוח במאה אחוז שיעבירו אותו דוקא למוסד של עכו"ם, או לא דתי, ובתבואות שור סי' ט"ו ס"ק כ"ד שכותב לדייק מדברי הגמ' הנ"ז דמשמע מזה דאין אזהרה דלפ"ע כי אם היכא דאיכא מכשול ודאי ע"ש, וכ"כ עוד פוסקים. נוסף על זה הרי הילד עד שיגדל איננו עובר עי"כ שום עבירה, וכשיגדל הרי יתכן גם שיחזירוהו למקום שיוכל לשמור על יהדותו. (יעוין שו"ת חתם סופר חאו"ח סימן פ"ג, וכף החיים או"ח סימן שמ"ג ס"ק כ"ב ע"ש).

אולם אם לא קיים חשש מבוסס ממשי של פיקוח נפש והשיקול הוא ביותר רק מה שטובת הילד, אז אסור להתלונן במשטרה כזה כאשר הסיכויים מבוססים שיוציאו עי"כ את הילד מבית הורי המסורתיים או הדתיים ויעבירוהו /ויעבירוהו/ למוסד עכו"ם, או לא דתי, או לא מסורתי, אם לא שהוריו המה ג"כ כבאלה, וכדאיתא בספרי פ' כי תצא עה"פ לא תתעב אדומי, שהמחטיא האדם קשה לו מן ההורגו, שההורגו אין מוציאו [אלא] מן העוה"ז והמחטיאו מוציאו מן העוה"ז ומן העוה"ב. וכך מצינו לחכמת אדם בכלל פ"ט סעי' י"ב שפוסק וז"ל: אין מוסרין תינוק ישראל לעכו"ם ללמדו ספר וללמדו אומנות, אפילו במקום דליכא למיחש לש"ד כגון במקום מעבר לרבים מ"מ אסור שמא

Child & Domestic Abuse

ימשך אחר מינות, ונ"ל דהוא הדין דאסור למוסרו לישראלים האפיקורסים דגרעי טפי מן הגוים דאפיקורס ישראל ממשיכים יותר עכ"ל, ודון מינה ומינה.

ב) ואבוא לשאלתו השניה שהיא: במקרה שהאב בא על בתו הקטנה פעמים חוזרות ואין כאן חשש של פיקוח נפש, מה הדין לגבי הספיקות שהעלתי לעיל.

והנה לדעתי הדין בזה כפי שהעלתי לעיל בשאלה הקודמת במקום חשש לפיקו"נ, כי הרי דין אחר הערוה כדין רודף אחר חבירו להרגו, והבא על בתו הרי הוא מחייבי כריתות, והגם שהיא קטנה אבל האב חייב על כך, ומן החובה איפוא להפרישו מזה, ויעוין במשנה למלך בפרק כ"ד מה' שבת הלכה ז' שחוקר גלל כן היכא מי שרודף אחר הערוה בשבת אם מחללים שבת בשביל להצלתן מן העבירה, וכן בספר מחזיק ברכה להחיד"א ז"ל או"ח סימן של"ט סק"ה שמביא בשם רבינו יונה שכתב דכל אותן שמצילין אותם בנפשם משמע דלא מפלגינן בין חול לשבת, וכזאת מביא גם בשם הכנה"ג ושו"ת יעו"ש ביתר אריכות. **וכל זה הוא נוסף למה שיש חיוב להציל את הקטנה מנזק פיזית ונפשית, ובהיות כ"ז יחד נראה לי דיש לפסוק כנ"ז בשאלתו הקודמת.**

ג) על המקרים האמורים בא כב' בשאלה נוספת בנוגע לדין מוסר, ומפרט וכותב, דבשאלה א' שמדובר על פיקוח נפש ויש לו דין רודף יהי' מותר למסרו אותו, אך מה יהא הדין בשאלה ב', הלא כותב השו"ע בחו"מ סי' שפ"ח סעי' ט' שאסור למסור "ואפי' היה רשע ובעל עבירות ואפי' הי' מיצר לו ומצערו", וא"כ האם מדובר גם על מקרה כזה כשיש נזק של ממש גם פיזית וודאי נפשית. וזאת תשובתי על זה, ראשית לדעתי כשם שברור לו בשאלה הא' שמותר למוסרו באשר כי הוא רודף, כך מאותו הנימוק מותר גם בשאלה הב', דהא היא ערוה עליו, ויש לו איפוא דין של רודף אחר הערוה וכנ"ל.

וזאת שנית, אפילו אילו לא היתה ערוה עליו שחייבים על זה כרת, ג"כ היה מותר למוסרו, הן כדי להציל אותה מפגיעתו בה, וגם לרבות, כדי להציל אותו מרשעתו זה, ומה שכבר' מצטט ממה שנפסק בחו"מ סי' שפ"ח סעי' ט' שאסור למסור אפילו הוא רשע ובעל עבירות, אין לו ענין לעל כגון נידוננו, דבשם אין המדובר היכא שבא הדבר כדי להציל אותו מרשעתו, אלא המדובר שרוצים למסור אותו בשביל דבר אחר ורוצים לנהוג בו זלזול בין שהוא רשע ובעל עבירות, ולכן אסור, אבל משא"כ בכגון נידוננו שהמדובר שרוצים עי"כ להציל שלא יוכל להוציא לפועל זממת רשעתו, ולכן שפיר מותר למוסרו.

אמרנו שמותר זה גם בכדי להציל אותה מפגיעתו בה, באשר כי אין זה דומה גם למה שנפסק בשו"ע שם שאסור אפילו היה מיצר לו ומצערו, דבכאן הרי פוגע עי"כ בגופה ובנפשה, ויעוין בשו"ע שם בסעי' ז' שנפסק ברמ"א די"א דאדם המוכה מחבירו יכול לילך לקבול בפני עכו"ם אע"ג דגורם למכה היזק גדול, והש"ך בסק"ק מ"ה כותב בכעין החילוק הנ"ז, דשאני היכא שמוסר כדי שלא יוסיף להכות דמותר ע"ש. ומקרה כזה שלפנינו הוא יותר גרוע מהכאה, וא"כ יכולים למוסרו הן מפני שזה דומה למכה, ועוד יותר מזה, והן כדי שלא יוסיף עשות זאת. ובית דין אביהם של קטנים.

ד) ומהאמור, הדבר פשוט כבר ממילא, שגם בשאלה הג' שמפרט כבר' במכתבו על מקרים ידועים של התעללות מינית של מורה בגן ילדים, שמותר למוסרו, ונלמד זה עוד בק"ו מכיון שהא המדובר גם באדם שמציר הרבים ומצערן בדומה להנפסק בחו"מ שם סעי' י"ב. וכפי שמציין לזה שפיר כבר' במכתבו.

Responsa & comments of Gedolim

ה) על כל האמור נראה לי להוסיף לשם הבהרה עוד שתי נקודות, והמה: - 1. בודאי שאלת כבר' בשאלה הנוספת בנוגע לדין מוסר היא לא בנוגע למסירה בערכאות של ישראל, דבכה"ג נראה דבודאי מותר מכיון שהמציאות היא שכהיום אין כח בי"ד לדון על כך, אלא כוונת שאלתו היא בנוגע למקרה של מסירה לערכאות של עכו"ם, וכמודגש באמת בחו"מ שם בסע"י ט' בלשון: אסור למסור לישראל ביד עכו"ם וכו'. ורק גבי מסירת ממון בידי אנס כתוב בסעי' ב' שם "בין אנס עכו"ם ובין אנס ישראל" ע"ש. 2. גם בערכאות של עכו"ם נראה שיש חילוק בזה בין מדינות פראיות לבין מדינות נאורות, וכדמצינו שמחלק בכזאת הערוך השלחן בחו"מ שם בסעי' ז', המעיר שם וכותב, שכל המדובר בדיני מסור בש"ס ופוסקים הוא בכגון מדינות הרחוקות שלא היה לאיש בטחון בגופו ובממונו מפני השודדים והאנסים הגם שנשאו עליהם שם משרה, כידוע גם היום באיזה מדינות מאפריקה וכו', משא"כ במלכי אירופא ע"ש, ומוכח מהערוה"ש שם שלא כוון בדבריו רק משום מלכות, כי מפרט והולך שם לדוגמא גם שמות של מדינות שהיו מרוחקים מרחק רב מאד ממקום מגוריו וממלכות שהיה חי בקרבה כדיעו"ש. כאמור כתבתי זאת לשם הבהרה כללית בנושא זה של מסור.

בשולי התשובה.

נוסף על האמור בפנים מעיקרא דדינא בזה בלמסור לערכאות של עכו"ם בנידונים האמורים, הנה בצורך השעה וברשות בי"ד יש מקום להתיר אפילו כשזה שלא מעיקרא דדינא היכא שאין אפשרות לבצע זאת בישראל. ומצינו שהשיב בכזאת בשו"ת מבי"ט (א:כב), דכותב וז"ל: נקרא נקראתי לבית הועד חכמי צפת ומנהיגיה על ענין יעקב שנזרקו בו מינות וכן אחר הזכור ונתננו רשות למנהיגי הקהלות שייסרו אותו על יד האומות ונחבש בידם וכו'.

ונתינת רשות זאת שכותב המבי"ט היתה שלא על פי דין ורק משום צורך שעה ומיגדר מילתא, וכדכותב המבי"ט להלן בדבריו: כאשר לאח"ז התחנן האיש שישתדלו להצילו מהתפיסה ואמרו לו הממונים שאם ברצונו לצאת מהתפיסה שיגרש את אשתו, ונתרצה לכך וסידרו הג"ד בביטול מודעות וכו', ולאחר מיכן כעבור מעט מהימים היה הולך האיש ומוציא לעז על הג"פ שהיה אנוס בנתינתו וכו', והשיב על זה המבי"ט וז"ל: היכי דהאונס היה על דבר אחר ורק כדי להנצל מהעונש גירש לא הוי עישוי, וה"נ אע"ג דלא היה הדין למסור ביד אומות העולם, כיון שהיה ברשות בי"ד ולצורך שעה משום מיגדר מילתא בדין קרינא ביה וכו'. ומסיים המבי"ט וכותב שנשא ונתן בזה גם עם המהר"י בי רב והסכים עמו יעו"ש.

הרי בהדיא בהמבי"ט שהמדובר היה בהיכא שלא היה שם בדין למסור אותו ביד העכו"ם והיה זה רק משום מיגדר מילתא ולצורך שעה, וברשות בי"ד, וא"כ נלמד מזה שפיר דגם כשהדבר הוא לא מן הדין מכל מקום אם הוא צורך השעה ומשום מיגדר מילתא מותר למוסרו בידי עכו"ם שיחבשוהו בתפיסה, וזה ברשות בי"ד, ואז בדין קרינא ביה.

ודון מינה איפוא במכש"כ דמותר למוסרו בעל כגון נידוננו שכפי שביארנו בפנים הוא ממש בדין לעשות זאת, וכדי למנוע מאיש כזה שלא יעשו על ידו מעשים אשר לא יעשו כאלה על להבא, ופשוט.

Made in the USA
Charleston, SC
12 January 2012